GHOSTS AND LEGENDS
OF
YORKSHIRE

Eagle's Crag above Lydgate, scene of various Hallowe'en hauntings

GHOSTS AND LEGENDS
OF
YORKSHIRE

Andy Roberts

JARROLD

About the author

Andy Roberts lives in Brighouse, West Yorkshire, and has been involved in researching and writing about strange phenomena and folklore since the 1970s. His previous books include *Catflaps: Mystery Animals in the North* (1986), *Strange Calderdale* (1992), *Phantoms of the Sky, UFOs: A Modern Myth* (with David Clarke, 1990) and *Heads and Tales* (also with David Clarke, 1992). In addition he edits the quarterly journal of UFO studies and investigation, *UFO Brigantia*, and is a regular contributor to the magazine *Fortean Times*. He is employed as a project worker for a housing association in Halifax.

Acknowledgements

The author thanks the following for assistance in the research and writing of this book: Paul Bennett for the use of his extensive library, David Clarke for his advice and attention to detail and Helen Roberts for making it possible.

Readers wishing to report experiences of strange phenomena or folklore traditions may contact the author at 84 Elland Road, Brighouse, West Yorkshire HD6 2QR.

Picture credits
Halifax Central Library (p. 21); Huddersfield Library (p. 17); Ilkley Library (p. 46); National Portrait Gallery (p. 24); National Trust (p. 33); Simon Roberts (pp. 2, 7); Sheffield Newspapers Ltd (p. 14). All other pictures by the author and Jarrold Publishing.

Front cover: *The Cow and Calf rocks, a site of prehistoric religious significance and, more recently, UFO sightings*

ISBN 0-7117-0592-5
© Jarrold Publishing 1992
Published by Jarrold Publishing, Norwich
Printed in Great Britain 1/92

Contents

Introduction . . . . *page* 6

The South Pennines. 16

West Yorkshire 29

Ilkley Moor 44

The Yorkshire Dales 51

York 65

North Yorkshire and the Moors. 75

Mystery Animals in Yorkshire. 85

East Coast 94

East Yorkshire. 106

South Yorkshire. 117

Bibliography 128

Introduction

At the Ivy House Inn at Holmfield in Yorkshire a brass plaque on the wall above their 'demon' chair warns: 'This chair is of doubtful origin. You sit in it at your own risk, as others have proved conclusively'. The locals won't. As one put it, 'You sit in that seat and you pop your clogs.' Landlord John English says: 'All the lads who have used that chair were fit fellows. The last seven knew its reputation and condemned it as nonsense. We went to their funerals.'

The above comes not from some seventeenth-century book of travellers' legends but from twentieth-century Halifax. It was taken from Lyall Watson's 1990 book *The Nature of Things,* and the 1976 legend is testament to the continuing power of belief in Yorkshire today.

Nor is it a solitary example. Legends like this are as commonplace in the county now as they were centuries ago. It seems that despite the veneer of a sophisticated technological society, powerful beliefs and superstitions still run through the lives of Yorkshire folk.

People holding so-called primitive beliefs such as this have lived in Yorkshire since pre-historic times, littering the landscape with ancient monuments, standing stones and other sites, which were once the focus of their beliefs and superstitions. These sites have not faded with time, but have become 'belief attractors' for later generations of Yorkshire folk, a fact evidenced by such stones as White Rock at Luddenden Dean in the Calder valley, where the boulder is painted white each May Day morning – a last vestige of the tradition of worshipping this ancient stone, under which a long-dead chieftain and his treasure are said to lie.

The topography of Yorkshire is rich and varied, with mountains and moors, rocky sea coasts, wide open plains, valleys and dense woodlands making up the county, and this has attracted a wide range of people to live and work here. The land and the occupations afforded by it have helped shape the beliefs of the people and

White Rock in the Calder valley, painted white every year on May Day morning

the ghosts and legends of the county in turn reflect its inhabitants' main concerns.

For example, the lore of the east coast teems with tales relating to fishing. Many of these would be meaningless to, say, a Dales farmer. Mention the word 'pig' to him and he would happily talk for hours about different breeds and their merits. But to say the same word to an east coast fisherman would be to bestow bad luck upon him, and to this day there are some who will not take to sea if the word 'pig' is mentioned in their presence prior to a voyage.

Once, long before Yorkshire existed as a separate geographical entity, the region was at the centre of a far older kingdom named Brigantia. This area was home to the Brigantes, a Celtic tribe, who in turn had succeeded the older peoples of the north whose origins are more distant and mysterious. These peoples' dwellings and religious monuments can be found on the moorlands to this day – ruined settlements, stone circles and cairns. Legends attached to these deserted and lonely places still hint at the type of rites practised there. Clues are to be found in places such as the Iron Age settlement on the slopes of Blue Scar above Arncliffe, where there is a standing stone with a hole in it through which the rising sun on Midsummer Day is supposed to shine.

Other remains that our distant ancestors left behind were treated with caution by the people who succeeded them; flint arrow heads, for example, were thought to be elf-bolts, left by a race of tiny people of fairy origin. These 'elf-bolts' were believed to have magical properties and were often used as charms to cure cattle of diseases; beyond Skipton there is even a hill, Elbolton Hill, named after such finds.

All these early inhabitants of the county were later overthrown by the Romans, who in turn were followed by Angles, Danes and Norse settlers. We can see the physical remains of these peoples in the artefacts they left behind, but what of their ghost stories and legends? None were written down, but by the spoken word and through one long intermingling of races and cultures, the exchanging and mixing of myths, folk tales, beliefs, customs, superstitions and religions, a large body of ghost stories and legends has reached us which stretches from prehistoric times to the present day.

Ghosts and legends are often dismissed by the sceptical as trivial, but they stem from people's deeply held beliefs and behind every tale there is a story of human experience waiting to be unearthed. It is unwise to mock that which is not understood and besides, would someone who sneered at any of the stories in this book be willing to risk sitting in the 'demon' chair at the Ivy House Inn, knowing its history?

Much is made of the study of history in Yorkshire in the form of buildings, trade routes, industry and so on, and this gives a picture of the secular, everyday life of inhabitants, past and present. But it tells us virtually nothing about what ordinary folk believed about the world they lived in.

Historians and archaeologists can tell us little about the giant standing stones at Boroughbridge, or the carved stone head above the Sun Inn at Haworth. But ask a local person and you will be given several answers and lines of further enquiry, richly laden with the folklore of the area which has been handed down over the years.

The study of belief and superstition, which can inform us about ghosts and legends, is usually ignored by historians, as if it were robots, people without feeling or imagination, who built the towns and roads, farmed the hills and dug lead from beneath them – and who ultimately created the monuments and folk tales from their beliefs and experiences. This is a very narrow way of viewing the past and we need to look beneath the surface of the everyday to a deeper, hidden history. We need an archaeology of belief and a new way of seeing to begin to explain these mysteries.

Being inextricably bound up in the beliefs of the people over many centuries, the ghostlore and legends of Yorkshire are equally intertwined with the various religions to which the county has played host. Prior to Christianity the indigenous peoples had a variety of religions based on pantheism (the belief that the universe itself is God), which merged with those brought across by invaders and settlers. These in turn later overlapped and mixed with the influx of Christian lore and legend, and the names of the various gods and spirits once revered can be seen in place names throughout the county, such as *Thor*ganby and *Fairy* Cross Plain.

The pagan religions were tolerated by the Church in an effort to absorb them. In a letter to St Augustine, Pope Gregory wrote:

The temples of the idols should on no account be destroyed . . . destroy the gods, but the temples themselves are to be sprinkled with holy water, altars set up and relics enclosed within.

Thus many old sites became part of the Christian Church and we can see this in several places throughout Yorkshire. The 'devil stone' built into the side of the church at Copgrove near Ripon was once part of an earlier faith's lore, and numerous churches such as those at Lastingham and Bradfield were built on prehistoric sites, already centuries old.

Other examples of this superimposition of belief systems and lore can be seen at Hinderwell on the east coast, where a holy well can be found in the churchyard. The old tradition of making and drinking liquorice water from the well there on Ascension Day is a Christianisation of the water worship which would once have taken place on 1 May, the old Celtic festival of Beltane.

No study of ghostlore and legend can be undertaken without

accepting that people's religious and spiritual beliefs, of whatever persuasion, have formed the basis for much of our folklore today.

One of King Canute's laws aptly defined these beliefs as being the worship of 'the sun or the moon, rivers, water, wells or stones or great trees of any kind', and we will see that a great many ghosts and legends concern themselves with just such sites or particular customs which are held at times of the year when the sun is in a certain position.

In later centuries the split between Church and country traditions became more pronounced, but for a long time the old ways ran alongside those of the new, sometimes with unexpected results. It was recorded in 1597 at Hunsingore church that:

Ffrancis Thompson and George Allan did in a most contemtuous manner bring into Hunsingore Church a Toie, called the Flower of the Well, in the time of Divine Service, wherebie the Vicar was disturbed.

This presumably good-intentioned effort of country folk to meld pagan water worship with divine service was not looked upon kindly, and the pair were punished by being stripped semi-naked and whipped through the streets of Wetherby.

Nowadays vestiges of paganism, such as well dressing and morris and sword dancing, are often carried out with the full sanction of the Church authorities, as at Handsworth near Sheffield, where sword dancers traditionally dance outside the parish church near the time of the winter solstice. Ghosts and legends are even mentioned in some church guides as an added attraction to interested visitors.

Certain themes are evident in any study of the folklore of Yorkshire. Ghost stories naturally remind us of our mortality, and the desire not to leave the material world seems to be so strong that thousands apparently come back as spirits. Ghost tales also indicate the lasting power of emotion and feelings, as many ghosts are those thwarted in love, or the victims of murder or tragic accidents.

When Yorkshire's ghostlore is examined closely the number of headless ghosts described is staggering, and sifting through the layers of belief which surround such mysteries we are taken back through time to a period when the human head was considered sacred. Skulls were once used as a protective symbol, and later heads were carved in stone. This was a time when heads were taken as trophies in battle and also for sacrificial purposes, and the severed head is a theme which recurs throughout this book.

Stone heads are found on buildings dating from the earliest houses to bridges and chimneys constructed within the past fifty years. Even the industrial town of Keighley has two chimneys with carved heads, said to have been placed on them by workmen to lay the ghosts of colleagues killed during the construction. Thus we enter the realms which some may call mere superstition. Others, who see the universe in a different way, however, would call it respect or prudence.

But superstition, if we call it that, still exists throughout the county, reminding us of our uncertainty and fear of the world which, despite the reassurance offered to us by television advertisers, is obviously no less strange to those people who now place a horseshoe above their door than it was to our Bronze Age ancestors, who peppered Ilkley Moor with strange cup and ring symbols.

People today attribute their superstitious activities to a search for 'luck'. A walk round any Yorkshire town or village will reveal numerous instances of the 'lucky' horseshoe, symbol of the Anglo-Saxon god Wayland the Smith, nailed above doors and windows – traditionally the place where evil spirits entered a house.

Many homes sport cartwheels on their walls or in their gardens yet few people know that they are an ancient symbol of the sun. Also it is still possible to find houses with anvils standing outside, another symbol of the god Wayland. All these artefacts hark back to a time when the universe was perceived to be alive, when the natural world and the landscape were both feared and celebrated – a time before, as the poet William Blake put it, our perceptions were dulled and we succumbed to 'single vision and Newton's sleep'. Now it appears we have the beliefs without the awareness of their origins and intent.

When viewed in this light, ghost stories, landscape legends and calendar customs can be seen as multi-layered experiences and events, informing us about the past from a different viewpoint and heightening awareness of ourselves and the world in which we live.

Even a 'simple' ghost story can tell us about the physical history of a landscape, the origins of a particular house and family, the psychology and sociology of the people who saw the ghost, and how it was reported in the media. As always, the mystery of the

Cottage at Fremington. Cartwheels, ancient symbols of the sun, are typically seen outside houses throughout Yorkshire

unknown remains to tantalise us, to hint that the universe may be, in the words of one famous physicist, 'not only stranger than we imagine but stranger than we *can* imagine'.

People often say, 'I don't believe in ghosts,' but these are invariably people who have never seen or experienced anything out of the ordinary. In our twentieth-century culture we use ghosts to frighten, but this is largely a received image, usually based on fictional ghost stories or films. There are, however, other sources available.

Take the experience of the folklorist S. Baring-Gould. While he was wandering across the lonely moors above Malham in 1867, darkness began to fall and he was in great fear of falling down one of the many pot-holes which pockmark the area. As he trudged warily through the landscape he was joined by a dark misshapen creature which walked with 'a wriggle and a duck accompanying each step'. Failing to make conversation with his ghostly companion, Gould accepted the situation and was content just to follow in the hope that he would be led to safety.

Suddenly, as he attempted to cross a stream, the ungainly figure, now some way ahead, flew back, plucked him from the stream and deposited him a hundred metres away, saving him from falling into a pot-hole. As he gathered his composure, Gould noticed his companion had slipped away down the pot-hole to be replaced by a flash of light which wavered and hovered, held in the hand of 'a young woman, the countenance wondrously beautiful, but full of woe unutterable'.

Gould fled from the spot, thinking he was hallucinating, but when he turned, there was the light and its bearer again. She beckoned to him to follow, which he did: 'I ran to catch her up, but the faster I pursued, the swifter glided the flame before me.' After several miles of pursuit both light and figure vanished and Gould could see before him safety in the form of a small hill farm. Upon his arrival the farmer told him that he had first seen the local boggart, followed by Peggy wi' t' Lanthorn.

Gould named this apparition the Boggart of Hellen Pot, 'boggart' or 'boggard' being a Yorkshire term for almost any undefined supernatural entity. But what was it really? Similarly, what exactly was the nature of his saviour, Peggy wi' t' Lanthorn?

How we interpret it depends upon the times in which we live. These days it would probably be seen as a 'white lady' type of ghost by traditional ghost hunters, a hallucination by sceptics, a UFO, or as some as yet unrecognised form of natural phenomenon. But, whatever the name given to it, for Gould the experience was objectively real and saved him from discomfort, if not actual death.

Few people now see fairies in the dell at Cottingley or hear the goblins knocking deep in the mines at Greenhow. But many have seen UFOs over Todmorden or experienced ghosts in haunted public houses. Mysteries are not something stuck in the past; today's mysteries are tomorrow's folklore, and Yorkshire has no shortage of developing ghost stories and legends. At the time of writing, a story appeared in the *Sheffield Star* of a luckless publican whose inn, the Carbrook Hall, has no less than four ghosts. Landlord Phil Skelton convincingly described the problems of living with so many phantoms:

> The most frightening experience was when something or someone brushed past me on the hallway. There was no one there that you could see but I felt a cold sensation and the hairs on my arm stood on end.

A modern ghost perhaps, but the effects on humans are timeless – in this case pure fear.

Crop circle discovered at Rotherham in July 1990

However, the deep mysteries of 'how' and 'why' remain, with explanations constantly sought to provide the curious with reasons for these apparent rents in the fabric of reality as we have been taught to understand it.

Crop circles are the latest manifestation of this process, with speculation about their causes ranging from the work of extra-terrestrials to that of fairies, from natural phenomena to hoaxes. These enigmatic rings have appeared in Yorkshire over the past few years, around Rotherham, and look set to become as frequent a visitor as the fairy rings once were to farmers in the Yorkshire Dales.

Perhaps it is how we perceive the world which helps us shape these events. Experiences of ghosts, UFOs, boggarts and the like *do* happen and it would be foolish to deny it, except to suggest that the witnesses perhaps may have been mistaken in their interpretation. When hundreds of people witnessed multi-coloured lights as large as a football field flying over Hull in the 1980s, they were convinced it was clear evidence of UFOs. When it was discovered that the 'UFOs' had been aircraft on refuelling manoeuvres, many refused to accept this explanation, and rightly so. They had undergone a UFO experience, a modern-day wonder, and who were the UFO investigators to take that away from them?

Rather than believe or deny any of these experiences we need to develop a new way of looking at the world, one which combines the acceptance of the experience with interpretation of the facts.

UFOs, now commonplace visitors to the county, were once never seen here. No one knew about the possibility of life on other planets and so UFOs could not possibly exist. But people did see 'dragons' in the sky and Will-o'-the-wisps on the moors – surely the same unidentified flying objects under a different name? Dragons too seem to have vanished from experience, and no longer are villages such as Handale terrorised by fire-breathing beasts which ruin the crops. But in their place we now have the mystery of the big cats which stalk unchallenged across the county, terrifying people and confusing the police.

This new way of seeing and dealing with such experiences is perhaps best summed up by the ghost writer Thurston Hopkins' comments on haunted houses and things mysterious in general. After a lifetime of investigating mysteries, he was still unsure where their origins lay. Loathe to dismiss people's experiences out of hand but equally unwilling to invest belief in 'things that go bump in the night', he said:

Of course I cannot prove that ghosts did appear there. Nobody can *prove* that. But I suspect these things; and pass along the borders of the world intangible, in lack of complete understanding, but not without a certain feeling of awe and bewilderment. Where the reader sees the world fair and common, I see the world a place of mysteries and miracles.

Finally, the 'demon' chair still exists at the Ivy House Inn. But a previous landlord took the warning plaque with him when he left and now the chair is regarded as just another seat in which to enjoy a drink. The people who sit in it still die, of course, but now of old age and natural causes rather than the effects of the chair. Belief in that particular mystery has gone and a different way of seeing has taken over.

The South Pennines

The landscape of the South Pennines comprises high moorland cut with deep valleys, dotted with hillside settlements such as Hebden Bridge. The weather at any time of year can be spectacular in its power, and the South Pennines are best evoked by walking a moorland trail at sunset, or by reading the works of Poet Laureate Ted Hughes, who once lived in Calderdale and wrote extensively about the land and its people.

Villages remained isolated here until comparatively recently. Celtic scholar Dr Anne Ross has said of the region: 'I had failed to realise that each mill-town and village was, almost to this day, largely cut off from the others and isolated. It is a treasure house of continuity.' Ghosts and legends are part of that continuity.

Castle Hill rises in the foothills of the Pennines and is visible for miles around in all directions. It is a deceptive hill, from the valleys looking like a towering mountain, although it is lower than the surrounding moorlands, while from the Pennine hills it appears to be a replica of Glastonbury Tor, complete with tower.

William Camden, the antiquary, wrote in 1586:

Near Almondbury, a little village, there is a very steep hill only accessible by one way from the plain; where the marks of an old rampart . . . and of a castle well-guarded with a triple fortification, are plainly visible.

The remains are those of an Iron Age hill fort, known to the Romans as Camulodunum, and it was this name which led some researchers to conclude that Camulodunum was the real Camelot, home of the warrior leader of Britain, King Arthur.

True or not, Castle Hill has borne this legend for hundreds of years, and many others which go some way to back it up. A battle was said to have been fought here in the remote past and archaeological excavation has discovered that the ramparts of the hill fort were burnt down, probably during a seige. Standing on the remains of the fortifications it is easy to imagine King Arthur defending the hill against the Saxon invaders during the final years of Roman occupation.

The Devil is also associated with Castle Hill, having once leapt to the summit from Scar Top at Netherton, eight miles away. The force of his leap left the imprint of his cloven hoof on the rocks at the Scar, visible to this day. Once on the hill Old Nick took to wandering the maze of subterranean caverns and passages said to lie beneath the mound, possibly in search of the legendary buried treasure – a golden cradle guarded by a great sleeping dragon, whose coils formed part of the hill itself.

King Arthur is not the only mythical figure to lay claim to this part of Yorkshire. For most people the name Robin Hood is inextricably connected with Nottingham and Sherwood Forest. His exploits as an outlaw fighting against the despotism of the rich and powerful are legendary, with thousands of people flocking yearly to locations in that area which are connected with him. Few realise that in Yorkshire there is a valley which has an equal if not greater claim on Robin Hood.

Robin may have been a flesh and blood outlaw to the people of Nottinghamshire, but in the Pennine valley of Calderdale he was that and much more. Local legends also see Robin as a giant

The unmistakable landmark of Castle Hill, viewed here from Ashes Lane

17

capable of enormous feats of strength, and the dale is littered with the remnants of his exploits. At Blackstone Edge, off the A58 trans-Pennine road, is an area named on maps as 'Robin Hood's Bed', where Robin the giant spent many nights slumbering on the boulder-strewn moors. His days were passed on the same spot, watching for enemies and practising his throwing skills. On one occasion he took a massive boulder from Blackstone Edge's shattered summit and hurled it into Lancashire, where it fell to rest on Monstone Edge, six miles away, and became known as 'Robin Hood's Quoit'.

Elsewhere in Calderdale Robin displayed his remarkable strength by throwing a monolith into the hills above Sowerby Bridge, where it became known as 'Standing Stone' and was subsequently used as target practice for his other missiles. From Standing Stone itself Robin threw a gigantic rock back across the valley to the hamlet of Wainstalls; the rock became 'Robin Hood's Penny Stone'.

There is another Robin Hood's Penny Stone, a huge natural gritstone boulder, high on Midgely Moor about two kilometres from the nearest road. Old beliefs die hard in the Pennines and coins can still be found on the rock. Place one there for luck and it is sure to have vanished by the following day, although whether taken by supernatural agency or a local farm child is debatable! The name may have some connection with the stones used for exchanging food for money during one of the many plagues which swept Britain in the Middle Ages, but it is too large to have been placed there by a man and would have been a hard task even for a giant.

Twenty metres to the south-west is the enigmatic Greenwood Stone. Boundary stone or relic of prehistoric worship, its origins are lost but its nominal connection with Robin Hood and his favourite places is obvious. On a clear day the scenery here is unsurpassed, and it is easy to imagine the giant Robin striding the moors in search of sport, or perhaps just gazing at the landscape. One local tradition claims that the sun sets over the Greenwood Stone at the winter solstice when observed from the Penny Stone. Try it and see.

The confusion in Calderdale as to whether Robin Hood was a man or a giant raises many questions which the proponents of Robin as historical figure have yet to answer satisfactorily. Was the name 'Robin Hood' just a name given to one of England's old

Old postcard showing the room at Kirklees Priory where Robin Hood is said to have died

gods who had been suppressed by the invasion of Christianity? Was he a god or spirit who inhabited the forest and the greenwood, constantly at odds with the established order in the form of the sheriff and later the Church? The name 'Robin Hood' is thought by some folklorists to be a corruption of 'hob' – a Scandinavian term for a fairy, or from 'Robin of the Woods', an old name for the horned god Cernunnos. The mystery remains.

So much for the mythical Robin – what of Robin Hood the flesh and blood outlaw? Calderdale has links with this aspect of the figure too. According to a fifteenth-century ballad, *A Lytell Geste of Robyn Hood*, Robin trekked from Sherwood Forest to Clifton-on-Calder to make the acquaintance of Little John, who was to be his sergeant-at-arms in many adventures. Ironically, on his way to meet John he must surely have passed Kirklees Priory, where he was later to meet his end in strange circumstances. The valley of the River Calder was where the mortal Robin returned to die or, as some say, to be murdered. The true events surrounding his death are now lost in time and clothed with mystery, but all the ballads and legends agree that being old and probably very ill, Robin made his final journey to Kirklees Priory on the eastern edges of Calderdale.

According to the *Sloane M.S.* of AD 1600:

> . . . he repayred to the Prioress of Kyrkesley which some say was his aunt, a woman skylful in physique and surgery; who perceyving him to be Robin Hood and waying an enemy he was to religious persons, tok reveng of him for her own howse and all by letting him bleed to death.

This action may seem strange, but bleeding was thought to be a cure for many ills in the Middle Ages, and it is not hard to imagine Robin letting this take place if he thought he was to be rejuvenated.

Proponents of Robin as a pagan woodland god see this account of his death as being indicative of the ultimate struggle between the old and new religions. Robin here is the dying god, triumphed over by the newly established Christianity.

By the time he realised he had been the victim of treachery it was too late, but rather than be buried at the hands of nuns, Robin marshalled his will-power and managed one final feat. Having summoned Little John by horn blast, Robin stood at the window with his support and drew his bow for the last time. Accounts speak of him turning to Little John, saying, 'Wherever this arrow lands, there shall I be buried.'

With his strength failing fast he fired the arrow and then, weakened by the loss of blood, Britain's most famous outlaw died. The arrow fell some 275 metres away, a magnificent bow shot for any man, not least someone on the verge of death. Free at last from the clutches of the sheriff and religion, Robin Hood was buried in the greenwood he knew and loved, his resting place marked by a simple stone on a trackway used by the countryfolk he defended.

But even in death Robin was still harassed by the rich and powerful. His original gravestone, said to be an ancient standing stone, was stolen by a local knight and used as a hearthstone in his manor. However, supernatural forces were at hand and the first morning after the theft the knight found it had been removed from the fireplace and 'turned aside'. This phenomenon took place three times, a magical number, after which the monolith was returned to the greenwood to mark the grave.

The local folk held this grave in great reverence for years to come. So much so in fact that in the nineteenth century it had to be fenced off to prevent people from taking chippings as a cure against toothache and other ailments.

There are few reminders now of Robin's last hours. The gate-house from which he fired his last shot is uninhabited and decaying, but the grave still exists to the west of the nettle-overgrown site of the priory. Surrounded by trees and dappled by sunlight in spring, it is perhaps a fitting resting place for possibly one of England's greatest heroes. Man or myth, no one will ever know the truth about Robin Hood. His memory lives on in Calderdale and the real question is not 'did he ever live?' but rather 'will he ever die?'

Halifax is infamous for being the only town in Great Britain to behead criminals with a guillotine, or 'gibbet' as it is known locally. A replica of the device still stands in Gibbet Street and criminals could be decapitated for what today would seem a minor offence. For instance, anyone caught stealing goods above the value of 13$^{1}/_{2}d.$ stood to lose his head. The first documented beheading took place in 1286, and between 1541 and 1650 at least fifty people were executed in this barbaric fashion. If the theft was of a farm beast then often the animal was attached to the releasing mechanism of the gibbet and encouraged to pull.

However, victims did have a way of avoiding this punishment. If they could remove their heads just as the gibbet's blade fell *and*

The notorious Halifax gibbet, seen here in a contemporary print

The Halifax gibbet, as it is today, in Gibbet Street

escape across the parish boundary at Hebble Brook never to return to Halifax, they were safe. Surprisingly, several people managed this feat, including one John Lacy, who foolishly returned seven years later – and was summarily beheaded. It did not pay to break the law in Halifax in those days and the 'Gibbet Law' was feared throughout the land. It became part of the thieves' litany: 'From hell, Hull and Halifax, may the Good Lord deliver us' – the reference to Hull being to the notorious prison there.

Further to the west, in the precipitous Cliviger Gorge, flying phantoms seem to be the fashion. High above the hamlet of Lydgate looms Eagle's Crag (see frontispiece), so-named because it strongly resembles an eagle's head and beak. UFOs have been sighted hovering above this rock and an older legend tells of a ghostly white doe seen around the crag each Hallowe'en, the result of a feud between a local huntsman and a witch. Loynd Wife, one of the celebrated but doomed Pendle Witches, also haunted the rock, using it as a lookout-post from which to spot her victims.

The gorge is home to the Gabriel Hounds, spectral presagers of death, which fly down the gorge and vanish into the earth near Mankinholes Youth Hostel on the Pennine Way, also on Hallowe'en. But the most mysterious of the aerial phenomena in the gorge has to be that which policeman Alan Godfrey encountered on the night of 28 November 1980.

Whilst searching for stray cattle on the outskirts of Todmorden in his panda car, Godfrey came across what he at first thought was an early morning bus. As he neared the object he realised with shock that the 'bus' was hovering above the ground. He attempted to contact his headquarters but neither band of his police radio would work and so, being a conscientious officer, he managed to keep calm long enough to sketch the object.

His drawing shows the UFO to be shaped somewhat like a toy spinning-top, with a row of windows splitting the object into two. The top part was stationary while the bottom was spinning in an anti-clockwise direction. As he could see his headlights reflected off the object, and the trees and bushes on either side of the road being blown about by the down-draught, he concluded that this was a real, solid object which could not be anything other than a UFO.

As he sat watching it, considering what to do next, he suddenly found himself a hundred metres down the road with no UFO in sight, unable to explain his sudden relocation in space. Returning to the police station he told a fellow officer of his experience and together they went back to the spot. Although there was nothing whatsoever at the scene of the close encounter, they noticed that the road at the spot above which the UFO had been hovering seemed dry in patches, in marked contrast to the rest of the road which was wet from the night's intermittent rainfall.

Others had also seen something in the air over the Todmorden area on that night. Twenty minutes before Godfrey's sighting three police officers on the moors ten miles away had spotted a blue ball of light descending into Cliviger Gorge, and a lorry driver had reported to the police a bluish-white object seen in the valley at Cliviger itself.

As the story unfolded over the next few weeks PC Godfrey began to recall snatches of a previously hidden memory. He remembered getting out of the panda car at one point, and also hearing a voice inside his head intoning, 'You should not be seeing this. This is not for your eyes.' A short period of time was also missing from his account of the event. Eventually, almost a year later, Godfrey underwent hypnotic regression by a consultant physician and psychiatrist who knew nothing of the UFO encounter, only that the police investigators wanted Godfrey to be taken back to that date and time. In this and subsequent hypnosis sessions the police constable revealed that in the missing period of time he had been beamed aboard a UFO where he met a tall robed man, who telepathically informed him his name was 'Josef', together with eight small robot-like entities. The video-tape of Godfrey undergoing these sessions is emotive and frightening, and clearly rules out a hoax. As the alien Josef approaches he touches Godfrey with his hands and Godfrey's last word is 'black'. A physical examination seems to have taken place then before Godfrey was deposited back to his panda car.

Emily Brontë, whose spirit roams Haworth village and surrounds

Alan Godfrey has never claimed anything other than the initial sighting of the UFO and states, 'I never consciously claimed to be abducted. What I said under hypnosis is a mystery to me.' But the last word must go to Dr Jaffe who conducted some of the hypnosis sessions, 'Something very mysterious has happened to this man. I am as mystified as anyone else.'

Few visitors to the Pennine Dales can or should avoid a visit to Haworth. Despite the increased tourism because of its Brontë connections, this little hillside village with its literary shrine of Haworth Parsonage accurately reflects the essence of an old Pennine moorland settlement, with its past still tangible in the steep streets and lanes.

The Brontë sisters and their family were only too aware of the pagan traditions and hauntings embedded in the wild surroundings. Emily Brontë, a keen observer of moorland life, wrote that the inhabitants of Haworth had '. . . puritanical tendencies, their code of living embraced a throwback to their Norse ancestors, and their religion did not work downwards into their lives'. Her dissolute brother Branwell also knew of the supernatural animals which foretold death and wrote, 'The Gytrash is a spectre . . . [and] mostly appears in the form of some animal – a black dog dragging a chain, a dusky calf, nay even a rolling stone.'

However it is Emily, the most famous of the family, who has remained in spirit to haunt Haworth. Her apparition has been seen in many places in the village, most recently in the 1960s at the Weaver's restaurant, where she appeared to the shocked proprietor climbing a long-vanished staircase to the bedrooms above.

Emily's ghost has also been spotted walking the old pack-horse route from Stanbury village to the farmhouse at Top Withens, which is said to be the inspiration for *Wuthering Heights*. Another track leading to Top Withens past the Brontë waterfall is also the haunt of a 'white lady' type of apparition thought to be Emily, not earthbound as are some ghosts, but there of her own choosing perpetually to wander the moors she loved.

As the Brontës noted, traditional superstitions linger in these wild Pennine dales and the old ways of dealing with supernatural phenomena are still practised when it becomes necessary.

The old Sun Inn is just metres away from the Brontë Parsonage – a typical old coaching inn until you look more closely. Just above the door is a strangely carved stone head. It was placed there in

Old postcard showing Top Withens, inspiration for Emily Brontë's
Wuthering Heights

The old Sun Inn, Haworth, bears a modern-day carved stone head to ward
off evil spirits

the early 1970s by landlord Rennie Hollings, who had recently bought the inn, to lay a ghost.

The apparition was of an old pack-horse carrier who, dressed in a long leather cloak, had silently haunted the pub for years. Mr Hollings had heard about the ghost from local people and decided to deal with it in the time-honoured Haworth tradition. Interviewed in the *Yorkshire Post* he said:

> I didn't want to put any of my customers off because eventually I hope to become residential. Anyway I've found a way to deal with any supposed ghost. I have had a carved stone head erected over the entrance porch. There is a local tradition that these were put on buildings when a workman had been killed on the site before it was completed and they are supposed to ward off evil spirits.

Another Brontë connection exists at Ponden Hall, which was the inspiration for Thrushcross Grange in Emily's *Wuthering Heights*. The ghost here is a shape-shifter, said to be sometimes that of a grey-haired, bearded old man who used to appear as a portent of death for the Heaton family who once occupied Ponden Hall. If he was seen at the top of the hill behind the hall with his lantern aloft, or climbing one of the trees in the walled garden, then a death was sure to follow shortly.

In its other guise the ghost appeared as a fiery barrel which rolled down the hill and along a track in front of the hall, stopping at the old bee-keeping 'hive holes'. A variety of that strange luminescent phenomenon, Will-o'-the-wisp or Peggy wi' t' Lanthorn, this fireball was accepted by the local inhabitants, recorded Halliwell Sutcliffe, 'as coolly as if it were no more than a cow running wild after calving time, or any other usual phenomenon of their lives'.

In the manner of all ghosts it was eventually laid. Halliwell Sutcliffe investigated the exorcism and found:

> They will tell you, minutely, how it was done. There was a man near Stanbury who understood the Black Art; they sought his aid, accordingly, against the spectre, and he waited on a certain winter's afternoon until the ghost appeared – in the grey beard's form this time. He lighted a rush-candle, and read the *Book of the Black Art* backwards, and held the candle in the phantom's face.

The ghost halted in its tracks at being challenged in this fashion and the wizard finished the job swiftly, saying, 'Niver come nigh th' owd house again til tha's seen this rushlight burn .to th'end', and with this he swallowed the burning candle ensuring that the ghost could not see it burn out. The spell being complete, the ghost vanished and was rarely seen again.

At 457 metres on Crow Hill is a solitary standing stone known as the Lad o' Crow Hill. On it are carved the confusing words 'Lad Orscarr on Crow Hill'. One version of the legend states that the stone is named after an orphan who was lost and died in the snow while tramping the moors. An argument ensued over whose responsibility the burial was. The parishioners of Stanbury and Haworth, although the body was on their parish, wanted no part of it and Trawden parishioners were equally reticent to move the corpse. Eventually Trawden parish took responsibility and at the same time extended its boundaries by erecting the stone.

Keighley poet Gordon Bottomley was so entranced by the story that he wrote 'For a Grave on the Moor' in commemoration of the unknown lad's final resting place:

Calmly I lie in heat and cold
In the new year, in the old.
Ashes to ashes, dust to dust,
Here I live, I have no lust;
Body rest in the upland bleak,
Forth I go old friends to seek.

West Yorkshire

The Three Nuns Hotel is well within bow-shot of Kirklees Priory where Robin Hood is said to have died, and although it is unconnected with the outlaw, during the summer of 1985 it was the focus of a supernatural visitation when renovation uncovered a strange carving of a horned ram's head. Almost immediately strange things began to happen. Site manager Ian Thompson witnessed unusual phenomena when he was alone in the pub waiting for a colleague. He heard doors slamming and footsteps going down into the cellar. In an attempt to rationalise this experience he shouted down into the cellar, certain another workman must have been there, but received no reply. Shortly afterwards he heard footsteps ascending the steps and doors once again banged open and shut. Finally, he went to investigate: 'I went into the cellar. It's always cool down there, but on that occasion there was a strange sort of chill about the place.'

The crossroads where the A58 trunk road bisects the A641 near Brighouse has been known as Hell Fire Corner for many years. The

The Three Nuns Hotel, where strange happenings followed the discovery of a carved ram's head during renovation work

name is often thought to be connected with the numerous serious road accidents which have occurred there, but it was actually known by that name before motor transport in the area was commonplace.

'Devil' names such as Hell Fire Corner often occur at locations which have a history of odd happenings and this spot is no exception, with its spectral headless horseman and tales of ghost cars appearing immediately prior to accidents.

Judy Woods, behind the crossroads, is also plagued by hauntings. Earth mysteries researcher Paul Bennett was confronted by some children in the woods in 1981, who told him of hideous white shapes floating between the trees. Later the same year, during a wave of UFO sightings, mysterious balls of light were seen flying over and rising from the woods together with strange craft entering and taking off from the trees. Towards the end of the spate of UFO sightings, a bus crashed at Hell Fire Corner and the driver later blamed the accident on a hovering UFO which momentarily distracted his concentration before the bus skidded out of control.

High Fernley Hall at Wyke has a long tradition of strange phenomena, which began during the eighteenth century when it was occupied by the Bevers brothers, both of whom were besotted by the same girl. After witnessing her marriage to his brother at Kirkheaton church on 5 May 1742, the rejected suitor rode to High Fernley and told the servants that some misfortune was going to befall him, but that he would 'come again' without his head. He then deliberately, but by means unrecorded, beheaded himself and true to his final words began to appear every night in the form of a headless horseman. His family left the hall in terror and it stood empty for many years, with few even daring to pass it at night, until that portion of the hall where the suicide took place was demolished, reducing the building to its present size.

The Brown Cow pub at Denholme was the scene of a very disturbing haunting in early 1990, when landlord Barry Ditmer and his family became the playthings of a powerful poltergeist-like ghost shortly after taking over the pub.

In a litany of ghostly happenings the Ditmers all experienced room temperatures dropping to freezing-point, smells of rotten eggs, tobacco smoke drifting through the rooms, and objects being moved by unseen hands in the beer cellar. Most frightening of all was when Barry Ditmer was thrown through the air by an invisible assailant. One attack was observed by barman Don Clancy who saw the landlord pinned to the floor as if being strangled. In a newspaper interview Don recalled how he attempted to help his employer: 'I tried to pull him up, but couldn't. His face was turning blue and he had indentation marks on his neck.'

Events became so bad that at one stage the entire family moved out and the brewery replaced them with a relief landlady. But she too was visited by the poltergeist and left in terror. The brewery took the haunting seriously enough to comment: 'Obviously the family is very upset by events and the brewery has tried contacting various institutes and universities for help, but to no avail.'

Bolling Hall at Bradford is now a museum but if its walls could speak they would tell of a terrible tragedy narrowly averted by a ghost. During the English Civil War Bradford was largely comprised of Puritans and was under seige, led by the Royalist Earl of Newcastle.

The Earl was angry because his friend, the Earl of Newport, had been killed while the seige was being laid. As a result he gave the savage order that his troops should 'put to the sword every man, woman and child, without regard to age or distinction whatsoever'.

But during the night before the massacre when the Earl was sleeping at Bolling Hall, he was woken three times by the bed-clothes being pulled from him. Each time he saw a pale, white-clad female spectre who implored him softly to 'pity poor Bradford'. Whether his mind was troubled enough by his draconian order to create an illusion or whether the spirits of the otherworld conspired to stop the slaughter we cannot know, but by morning he had changed his mind and the people of Bradford were saved.

Calverly Hall near Shipley was the home of Walter Calverly during the sixteenth century. He was a wild, free-living man who slowly squandered the fortune left to him by his father, resulting in creditors and money-lenders closing in on him. This, coupled with the pressures of his jealous wife, seems to have driven him insane in 1604.

On 23 April of that year his mind snapped and he attacked his family, killing two of his children and leaving his wife for dead. He then rode off to slaughter his other child who was staying with a nanny but before he could carry out further parricide he was captured and eventually taken for trial at York.

His sanity appears to have returned momentarily at the trial and he refused to plead – an action which ensured his remaining possessions would be passed on to his surviving child, but which earned him a horrible death. The penalty for refusing to plead in those days was *peine forte et dure* or death by crushing.

Calverly's body was secretly brought back to the churchyard at Calverly to rest amongst his ancestors, but his tormented spirit took to riding through the outskirts of Bradford on a headless steed. The ghost was exorcised by the Vicar of Calverly and banished 'for as long as the hollies grow green in Calverly Wood', but the hauntings continued. Demonologist Eric Maple commented:

> The ritual was singularly unsuccessful which suggests that the rites of exorcism, whilst usually effective in coercing the spirits of sane men, can have little influence or none when the ghost is mad.

In a sober but terrifying account the Revd Richard Burdsall described how he was visited by the Calverly ghost when he stayed at the hall. Immediately after he dropped off to sleep, he was hurled out of bed by an unseen force. This indignity took place twice more and the clergyman was so frightened that he got up at one o'clock and spent the rest of the night in prayer.

The ghost both terrified and fascinated local inhabitants and a ritual was devised to call the ghost up. In a manner suggestive of a witches' coven, twelve people would meet near the church and make the shape of a pyramid on the ground with their caps. Following this they would form a circle and dance round singing:

> *Old Calverly, old Calverly, I have thee by the ears;*
> *I'll cut thee into collops unless thee appears.*

As the rhyme was chanted breadcrumbs mixed with pins were scattered on the ground and those who dared would whistle through the church door keyhole. Usually, however, those participating in this rite would flee at its completion rather than wait around to see if they had been successful.

East Riddlesden Hall on the A560 near Keighley is now owned by the National Trust and it is an excellent example of seventeenth-century architecture and decoration, with the additional attraction of one of the finest medieval barns in Yorkshire. The hall sports more than its fair share of ghosts, with at least five apparitions having been seen over the years in either the hall or grounds.

The most famous is the 'grey lady' who is seen wafting up and down the corridors seemingly with no particular purpose or destination. One legend claims that she was a former owner of the hall who was caught with her lover in a somewhat embarrassing situation when her husband returned unexpectedly.

In a reworking of this time-worn story, instead of murdering either one outright, the cuckolded husband locked his wife in the bedroom and bricked her lover up alive in a corridor wall. Naturally they both starved to death but curiously only the wife returned to haunt her former love-nest – and at least she was in one piece. Her lover is said to appear only as a disembodied head at the window of the wall he was bricked up in, and in support of this tale a rumour exists that a male skeleton was in fact discovered in the wall many years ago.

The wooden cradle at East Riddlesden Hall is said to be rocked by an unseen hand each New Year's Eve

Nothing, however, remains of the Scotsman once murdered here except his ghost, most often seen near the window over the front porch. Accounts vary as to exactly who he was, but most say that he had travelled to Bingley in connection with the wool trade whereupon he took shelter at the hall in a blizzard. He was given hospitality and eventually shown to his bed in the room situated over the front door. The steward had got wind of the small fortune the Scotsman was carrying, however, and informed his master; between them they murdered the itinerant Scot during the night. As is often the case the murder was discovered and the steward was tried and hung at York for the deed in 1790. The master must have pulled the necessary strings though, as he got off 'scot-free'.

Other ghosts include a 'white lady' apparition, also said to be a previous owner, who vanished while out riding. Some say she was thrown into the hall's lake where she drowned, as her ghost is most often seen in the vicinity of the pool. The pool is also the spot where a ghostly coachman is sometimes seen, having inadvertently driven his team into the lake. Additionally, a cradle in one of the bedrooms has been seen to rock of its own accord on New Year's Eve. This plethora of ghosts must surely make East Riddlesden Hall one of the most haunted dwellings in the whole of Yorkshire.

Sixteenth-century Ryshworth Hall at nearby Bingley hit the headlines in November 1990, when owner Michael White claimed

Ryshworth Hall, where the unearthing of a mysterious stone head in the garden brought a run of bad luck

that a curse had befallen his family after they had unearthed a strange stone head in their garden.

Following the head's discovery in 1985, the White's luck changed dramatically. Alison White was struck down with an unexplained illness which left her weak and debilitated, and her husband's building business later collapsed. In desperation they gave the head to a sceptical friend, only to be dismayed when he went bankrupt shortly afterwards. Then the Whites' two daughters began to experience ghostly phenomena in their bedrooms, and Mrs White encountered a disembodied hand just as she was preparing to switch off an upstairs light.

These events led the Whites to try to sell the old hall in an attempt to change their luck, and the story of the haunted head came to the media's attention, featuring in many regional newspapers. The head was also put up for sale by auctioneers, who claimed it 'almost certainly originated in Celtic Britain'. Carved stone heads feature strongly in the folklore of northern England, but rather than bringing bad luck they were usually carved to avert it. When informed of this Mr White was unimpressed, saying:

If it is supposed to have brought good luck, goodness knows what would have happened to us if it was supposed to bring bad luck. The mouth on the head is carved in the shape of a smile but I always thought it was an evil sneer.

Despite, or perhaps because of, the publicity gained by the stone head's exposure in the press, the Whites failed to sell the hall and their luck remained unchanged. Even the carved head only raised £180 at auction, well below the hoped-for £300.

But there was quite a twist in the tail of this particular ghost story. Following the newspaper stories a Halifax woman contacted the *Yorkshire Post* and told them that the 'Celtic' head had in fact been carved in 1978 by her father William Hodgson, a previous occupant of Ryshworth Hall. He buried the head beneath the sycamore tree in the garden, telling his daughter it would confuse future archaeologists. Mrs Jones was highly amused by the Whites' story and dismissed all supernatural connections with the head, commenting that her father would be 'sitting on his cloud rocking with laughter'.

The auctioneers were equally shocked, a stunned spokesman for their Harrogate office saying, 'Carved in 1978? How awful!' That the actual age and origin of the head had no bearing whatsoever on the subsequent stories shows a great deal about how ghost stories and legends develop. The crucial thing was what was *believed* about the head and that, coupled with wishful thinking, auto-suggestion and fear, did the rest.

From the first day Gwen Morley came to work at a Keighley wool mill in 1925 the looms began to break down for no reason at all. Things became so bad that on 4 November the mill manager was called in to investigate. He had mechanics check the machines but still they mysteriously broke down until, that is, Gwen was removed from the room. The events came to the attention of the mill-owner who summoned Gwen to see him in a room containing fully operative singing jennies. The hard-nosed Yorkshireman was astonished at what took place. As Gwen walked towards him through a gap in the frames – hands in pockets so there could be no chicanery – all the wool ends snapped as she passed. Still doubting, the owner sent Gwen into another room which was spinning heavier yards, but again the ends snapped and the machines once more ground to a halt.

Gwen Morley seems to have been one of the people who possess what writer Charles Fort named 'wild talents': the ability to affect machinery and the outside world in some supernatural way. Mystified but more interested in profit than the paranormal, the mill-owner banned Gwen from working in the spinning-sheds and she was moved to the kitchens. This made no difference to her newfound abilities and the canteen was constantly disturbed by moving pans, falling crockery and shifting tables whenever Gwen was present. Over a three-day period in April 1925 twenty-three separate unexplained incidents were recorded and she was sent home from work.

The name Cottingley may ring some bells in the minds of travellers who see it signposted on the A650 road from Bradford, and so it should, for the tiny village was the scene of one of the most puzzling episodes in the history of the paranormal.

It began in the spring of 1917 when cousins Frances Griffiths and Elsie Wright started to pester their family with tales of fairies at the bottom of the garden. In an adult effort to demonstrate that fairies really don't exist Elsie's father gave her a camera and told her to prove it. No one was more shocked than he when thirteen-year-old Elsie and ten-year-old Frances brought the camera back with one photographic plate depicting Elsie surrounded by the little people.

Other fairy photographs were taken in the dell at Cottingley and the case became a worldwide sensation involving the paranormal investigator and *Sherlock Holmes* author Sir Arthur Conan Doyle, who pronounced the photographs authentic. Controversy raged over the years as to just how genuine they were, but no one could prove conclusively that they were a hoax. Throughout that time the cousins stuck to their original claim that the fairies were real.

Eventually, due to the persistence of investigator Joe Cooper the case was solved. 'There are things you should know,' Frances told him in a 1981 telephone call, and he travelled to her home in Ramsgate where she revealed that the photographs *had* been faked, using cut-out figures attached to bushes by hairpins. Such a simple technique had fooled experts for over sixty years. It was all over. Or was it? Despite the end of the case being trumpeted in *The Times* as 'Cottingley Fairies a Fake, Woman Says', the now triumphant sceptics missed something crucial in their self-congratulatory backslapping.

Although the cousins were now prepared to come clean as to how they had fooled the world, they were in dispute between themselves about the fifth picture which Frances claims to show a genuine fairy. The rest of the photographs were seemingly faked to prove to adults that fairies did really exist, but even after the hoax disclosures in the early 1980s the cousins insisted they had really seen fairies at the dell in Cottingley all those years ago.

The fairy tale does not end there. Others have come forward in support of Elsie and Frances to say that they too have seen fairies in the woods at Cottingley, and a carved stone was the focus for yet another fairy visitation at Cottingley. As nineteen-year-old Anne Freeman passed the impressive but little-known Bronze Age cup and ring carved boulder known as the Faerie Stone, she rested for a while on a stile. Her rest was almost immediately disturbed by a loud chattering from beneath her feet in a cleft between two rocks. The unintelligible jabbering came from two denizens of the fairy world, each 25 centimetres tall and dressed, as Anne put it, 'in what looked like medieval peasant dress'. As she stared in wonder the red-clad elementals ducked under the rocks and were gone.

Hawksworth Hall, to the north-east of Cottingley, was once visited overnight by James I. The old hall has had three ghosts in

The Faerie Stone at Cottingley – entrance to a fairy world?

the course of its chequered history. One, the spirit of a long-dead Negro servant or page-boy, was wont to creep into visitors' bedrooms whilst they slept to leave the imprint of his hand on their pillow. As is traditional with most old halls a 'grey lady' haunted the corridors, in this instance causing a nuisance by leaving doors open, and there are rumours that the faceless figure of a hooded monk has been seen walking in the hall and its grounds.

Kirkstall Abbey at Leeds has legends of ghosts and of a supernatural treasure-guardian. The abbey was built in 1152 by monks of the Cistercian order and was eventually left to decay during the dissolution of the monasteries in 1540. The original gate-house which stands across the main road is now the abbey's museum, home also to a ghostly abbot and poltergeist-like noises. In the seventeenth century a farmer working in fields near the abbey took a walk round the ruins in his lunch break. During these wanderings he discovered a hole in the ground which he had not previously seen. Cautiously, he entered the hole which widened into a passage leading him under the abbey to a vast subterranean room.

The room was illuminated by a roaring fire and in the far corner stood a black stallion, behind which the farmer could just make out a huge wooden chest surmounted by a black cockerel. Sensing that there would be treasure in the chest he made a grab for the lid, but as he did so the cockerel screeched and he was felled by a blow to the head. When he came round, the room had gone and he was lying stunned on the abbey's lawns. The legend seems to suggest that the 'room' only existed in the farmer's mind, and he entered it during some form of altered state of consciousness at what could be a power spot. This is a location where 'earth energies', perhaps in the form of a magnetic anomaly, are strong enough to affect the human mind.

Among the underground passages rumoured to exist beneath the abbey, one is said to run to beneath the City Varieties theatre on the Headrow in the centre of Leeds, home of the famous television show 'The Good Old Days'. Originally part of the White Swan pub, it became transformed into the north's leading music hall during the 1860s. It was rumoured that King Edward VII gave it his patronage in 1898, but in disguise, when he came to see his paramour Lily Langtry who was appearing there. Music hall legend alleges that the coat of arms above the proscenium arch was given by the amorous King after his visit.

Visitors, staff and actors at the theatre have reported three ghosts over the years. One, thought to be an actress, was seen by television producer Len Marten, who was accidentally locked in the theatre overnight. As she appeared in the room where he was

Kirkstall Abbey at Leeds, rich in ghosts and legends

dozing, the temperature plummeted and the producer shouted in terror when he saw her, causing the apparition to fade away into the fire. She was also seen by theatre-goer Elsie Cromwell, who came across the ghost in the ladies' room just as the theatre was closing in 1921. Thinking she was just another member of the audience, Elsie began to chat about the evening's show to the figure who was hunched over a wash-basin. Receiving no answer to her questions about the night's show, Elsie tapped the woman on the shoulder and almost fainted as her hand went straight through the old-fashioned clothing and on to the basin. Elsie said:

As I gasped for breath the figure turned and I could see straight into her eyes. She had a sad, pained expression and before I could do anything she walked past me and straight through the wall. The room was absolutely ice cold and I was terrified.

Temple Newsam House, known as the 'Hampton Court of the North' and originally owned by the mysterious Knights Templars, is no longer inhabited but is now a museum and art gallery attracting thousands of visitors a month. Its ghosts no doubt carry on haunting regardless, but when it was inhabited they were all seen on a regular basis.

The famous writer of ghost stories, Lord Halifax, actually lived at the hall until the 1920s and personally witnessed the 'blue lady' in 1908, when she walked across his firelit bedroom and through the wall into the adjoining damask dressing-room. Besides the ghostly screams emanating from the Red Room and the sounds of heavy objects being dragged across the floor from bedroom number four, the house is home to a ghostly infant who pops out from a cupboard, a ghostly Knight Templar and a ghost mist which inhabits the Long Gallery and can take the form of a variety of humans.

Leeds is justly famous for its medical school, but probably few of the students are aware of the origins of one of the skeletons preserved there, that of the 'witch' Mary Bateman. Whether or not she was actually a witch is open to conjecture but Bateman made a handsome living tricking people out of their money. Her most famous ruse was displaying a hen which laid eggs inscribed with the words 'Christ is coming', but her skulduggery was eventually to be her downfall. In 1809 she inadvertently poisoned Rebecca Perigo, one of her clients, with a 'magic' potion and was tried and hanged at York for murder. As was the custom, the body was later brought back to her home town and gibbeted; ghoulish locals took pieces of her skin to use as good luck charms before the medical school claimed her skeletal remains.

When Leeds was less built-up and the countryside encroached on to the town, the ubiquitous ghost dog was common in the area. Locally it was known as 'padfoot'. In 1866 folklorist William Henderson described the Leeds padfoot as:

> . . . about the size of a small donkey, black, with shaggy hair and large eyes like saucers; and it follows people by night, or waylays them in the road which they have come to pass . . .

The locals regarded it with terror, often staying at home on wild windy nights to avoid encountering the creature, a meeting with which would ensure a forthcoming death. Sally Dranfield from Leeds claimed to have seen it on numerous occasions, 'rolling along the ground before her, like a woolpack – sometimes vanishing suddenly through a hedge.'

Lumb Hall, a seventeenth-century house at Drighlington between Bradford and Leeds, stands back off the road, almost hidden by trees. However, if you walk up the narrow road at the side it is possible to gain a view of the outside and see a carved stone head above the door.

The mysterious 'Charlie' was once a frequent caller at Lumb Hall, Drighlington

41

Oakwell Hall bears the bloody footprint of a tragic seventeenth-century ghost to this day

It is not known whether the head was put there to lay the ghost which has been seen and heard at the hall, but Charlie, as the unearthly occupant is known, is fond of trying to attract attention by making a shuffling noise at the front door. Previous owners of the hall soon tired of finding no one there when they went to investigate and eventually learned to ignore the attention-seeking ghost.

Ghost-hunter C.T. Oxley, in his book *Haunted North Country*, relates an experience in which the sister of the hall's owner awoke one night to see a cloaked apparition rising through the air and up through the ceiling. It was later discovered there had once been a staircase to the room above. The cloaked spectre was assumed to have been an English Civil War ghost, and this theory was further strengthened in 1948 when a number of swords and weapons from that troubled period of history were discovered behind a wall panel.

Oakwell Hall near Birstall dates from Tudor times and was used by Charlotte Brontë as the model for Fieldhead in her novel *Shirley*. On 30 December 1684 it was the scene of a crisis apparition, when the Batt family saw their son William ride up to the hall and without speaking rush up to the main bedroom, whereupon he vanished, leaving only a bloody footprint as evidence of his passing. His family was later informed that he had been murdered that very day in Barnet, London, and it was his ghost at the time of death that they had witnessed. How a ghost can leave a bloody footprint is anyone's guess, but the mark remains to this day and Batt's ghost has been seen stalking the hall and gallery in an agitated state.

In the churchyard of St Peter's at Birstall grows a thorn tree, said to be a Glastonbury thorn, a direct descendant of the Holy Thorn at Glastonbury which flowers on Christmas Day. The original thorn sprang up when Joseph of Arimathea was giving a sermon on the birth of Christ and stuck his staff into the ground in affirmation of his religious faith. The staff immediately became a tree and flowered henceforth every Christmas Day from then on. The thorn in the churchyard at Birstall is recorded as having flowered on Christmas Day in 1782.

Nearby Horbury also had its ghost dog, one account of which tells what it must have been like to encounter this supernatural terror. One Horbury man saw the dog and in terror:

. . . struck at it, and the stick passed through it. Then the white dog looked at him and it had 'great saucer e'en'; and he was so flayed that he ran home trembling and went to bed where he fell ill and died.

Ilkley Moor

Ancient man used Ilkley Moor as a place on which both to live and worship and it is littered with relics of his passing, from the remains of Bronze Age field systems to the undeciphered 'cup and ring' carvings. On the summit of the moor alongside the prehistoric Rombals Way track is the Twelve Apostles stone circle. Actually consisting of thirteen stones, the name was superimposed on the circle to disguise its pagan origins, and legend says it is impossible to count the stones correctly at the first attempt. From here the Wild Hunt, dead souls led by the Devil, were said to fly out across the moortops in search of victims, and fairies have also been witnessed at the circle.

More recently UFOs have been seen at the Twelve Apostles, and in the summer of 1976 members of the Royal Observer Corps engaged on manoeuvres witnessed a bright white object float over the moor and hover above the circle. Ufologists have noted the frequent connection between sacred sites and UFO manifestations, and this, together with the proximity of UFOs and 'spooklights' to geological fault lines, has made Ilkley Moor a focus of UFO activity and interest for many years.

UFOs have also frequently been sighted at the Cow and Calf rocks (shown on front cover) in the form of small balls of orange light. Perhaps the best sighting of this nature took place on 26 September 1982, when some Ilkley women saw a bright glow above the rocks caused by the descent of two luminous balls of light, which hovered for a time before descending behind the rock outcrop.

The name Ilkley Moor is of recent origin and old maps usually refer to it as Rombalds Moor. In Norman times Robert de Romille owned the area and some scholars attribute the name to him, while others are equally convinced that the name arose from the pious Christian martyr St Rumold who died in AD 775. But folklorists are far more inclined to believe the name stems from the ancient legend of Rombald the stone-throwing giant.

That the old inhabitants of Ilkley Moor held stones to be of great significance and worthy of worship is evident in many of the moor's landscape legends. Long before man, the giant Rombald and his wife lived there – peacefully until they had an argument which led to Rombald storming off across the valley to Almescliffe Crag. Enraged by this untimely departure his wife gathered stones in her apron to hurl at him, but the strings broke under the weight and the stones fell, forming Great and Little Skirtful of stones.

In fact these piles of stones are Bronze Age burial barrows, and E.T. Cowling, author of *Rombalds Way*, speculated that this legend, one of many similar ones throughout Yorkshire, is:

. . . a record that these two barrows were made at a time when worship of the Mother Goddess was gaining ascendancy over that of the Sun God during Mid-Bronze Age times.

Perhaps it was sun worship which led the unknown carvers to chip out the famous Swastika Stone on the east side of the moor above Hebers Gill. The Swastika Stone can be seen as the symbol of all that is mysterious and strange about the moor, and in his book *Brigantia*, Guy Ragland Philips says of the carving:

Nobody could mistake it for anything other than a religious symbol. Within that limit various interpretations have been put on it – fire, or the sun, are favourites – but nobody knows . . . The motif is not primitive, but full of power.

The giant Rombald left other landmarks on the moor too. According to legend the Cow and Calf rocks were once one huge rock, until Rombald split them in one of his great strides to Almescliffe Crag. The rock basins on Almescliffe are said to be the footprints he made as a result of these leaps.

The Cow and Calf rocks were originally attended by the Bull, a rock as big as a cottage which has long since been broken into stone for roads and local buildings. Just as they are now a magnet for picnickers, walkers and climbers, the Cow and Calf rocks have attracted many legends over the years. The name suggests that this may even have once been a site for prehistoric religious ceremonies, as both cows and bulls were favourite objects of sacrifice amongst the Celtic peoples, and the tops of the nearby Hangingstones rocks are covered with some of the finest and most enigmatic cup and ring markings in the region. Part of Hangingstones rocks is named the 'Fairy Parlour', due to the belief that fairies occupied a hole in the rocks here.

Author Nicholas Size found Ilkley Moor to be such a powerful place that he experienced 'time-slips' here. On one occasion Size felt strangely compelled to visit the Cow and Calf rocks, where he went into a trance-like state and could see ghostly figures dancing around a fire. These figures were dressed in animal-skin cloaks and were enacting some kind of sacrificial ceremony.

Size was convinced that this was a vision of a ritual conducted here thousands of years ago, and he began to call the Cow and Calf rocks 'the Place of Horror'. Stranger still was the fact that Size 'saw' the Cow and Calf rocks as one large rock, which, as stated above, may formerly have been the case.

In a further experience with ghosts on the moor, Size again found himself watching a sacrifice. 'You are not real,' he cried out to the swirling figures as he tried to escape, but he was rooted to the spot, his mind in a whirl and his limbs controlled by forces beyond his comprehension. He wrote, 'My hands and feet seemed to be fastened in some way, and I was hauled and lifted hither and thither by hands which were irresistible.' Eventually he was able to tear himself free from the grip of the past, but afterwards felt as though he had been granted a vision of something he should not have witnessed, and that something had been 'implanted in [his] head by the power which was drawing him on'.

White Wells stands out clearly above Ilkley on the hillside and is easily reached from Wells Road. Once used as a bath house in the

White Wells, now a museum and tea room, was formerly the scene of fairy visitations

days when Ilkley was a celebrated spa resort, the building is now a small tea room and museum. Inside, water still gushes into one of the old plunge baths from an ancient Romano-Celtic stone head. When Size visited this spot he was filled with terror, feeling as though he should run from the area, although he didn't know why. The area of land to the east of White Wells was once known as the Fairies' House or the Fairies' Kirk, and the little people play a strong part in White Wells' past history.

It was said that in Saxon times a church was commissioned to be built on the site of the Fairies' Kirk, no doubt to quell vestiges of pagan belief at the location. But despite repeated attempts, the power of the fairies was too much for the Christian incomers and the builders found their construction materials were magically transported back into the valley so many times that they eventually gave up the struggle, and left the White Wells area to its otherworldly denizens.

The fairies were still there in the nineteenth century as keeper of the wells, William Butterfield, found out. One morning, instead of turning and unlocking the door as usual, his key seemed to be made of rubber, turning and turning with no effect. Withdrawing it to see if it was broken or if he had picked up the wrong key by mistake, he noted that it 'was the same that he had on the previous night hung up behind his own door at home'.

Abandoning the key altogether he tried to push the door open but only succeeded in having it repeatedly slammed shut by something inside the building. Eventually he forced the door open, to be greeted by a sight which few mortal men have ever seen. His experience was described in the *Folklore Record* for 1878:

Then, whirr, whirr, whirr, such a noise and sight! All over the water and dipping into it was a lot of little creatures, all dressed in green from head to foot, none of them more than eighteen inches high, and making a chatter and jabber thoroughly unintelligible . . . They seemed to be taking a bath, only they bathed with all their clothes on. Finding they were all making ready for decamping, and wanting to have a word with them, [Butterfield] shouted at the top of his voice – indeed, he declared afterwards he couldn't find anything else to say or do – 'Hallo there!' Then away the whole tribe went, helter skelter, toppling and tumbling, head over heels and all the while making a noise not unlike a disturbed nest of young partridges.

These days people rarely see fairies, but strange creatures from time and space still haunt the moor area in a different guise. Just above White Wells is a series of old stone quarries, where in December 1987 an ex-policeman had a classic close encounter of the fourth kind – the term used by ufologists to denote the abduction of a human being by UFO occupants.

While taking an early morning walk across the moor to visit his father in Morton, Philip Shaw was climbing the hill above White Wells when he heard a faint humming sound and in the quarry entrance saw 'what I can only describe as a small green creature moving quickly away'. Luckily, he managed to take a photograph of the creature before it disappeared into a small hollow.

Philip followed and as he rounded the corner he saw a flying saucer nestling in the bottom of a crater. He described it later as being 'like two silver saucers stuck together edge to edge with some sort of box sticking out of the top of the object that was descending into it'. While he stood, amazed, the humming increased and the UFO lifted off, vanishing before he could take another shot.

When he returned to Ilkley he found that a period of almost two hours had been 'lost' and later enquiries by a UFO investigation group led to his undergoing hypnotic regression, from which a story emerged about what apparently took place in the two hours of 'missing time'. It seems that Philip had been taken on board the UFO and out into space and back, and that the photograph had been taken *after* he had disembarked from the craft.

The film was developed, and among shots of local buildings and landscapes was a photograph of a small green figure in the quarry. Is this indisputable evidence of aliens from outer space? It may be, as all photographic analysis of the alien picture has suggested that it is a genuine humanoid figure on the film, and a hoax has been ruled out.

A long-standing tradition in the Ilkley area spoke of a 'lost' stone circle in the area between White Wells and the Cow and Calf rocks. Although archaeologists had dismissed the idea as fanciful, in 1885 the Revd Robert Collier wrote:

There was still a rude circle of rocks on the reach behind the old White Wells fifty years ago, tumbled into such confusion that you had to look once, and again before you saw what lay under your eyes; the stones were very large, and there was no trace of line about them, and this may have been a rude outpost of the tribe for the defence of the great living spring, and also of Llecan [Ilkley], lying below.

The circle was finally rediscovered when local man Nigel Mortimer located it at the head of Backstone Beck, near an ancient sheepfold. What makes this discovery remarkable is that he found the site by using a dowsing (water divining) technique. Where archaeologists with modern equipment had failed it seems that an innate human sense had succeeded.

Still more remarkable is the series of apparitions that Paul Bennett and Andy Tyson witnessed at the Backstone circle. In an experience similar to that of Nicholas Size (of which they knew nothing), the two men saw people walking in and out of the stones in a winding, ceremonial fashion. The ghostly celebrants speeded up their dance until they were a blur and could not be seen, a cone of energy forming in their place. This spinning vortex vanished, to be replaced by flickering bands of light on and around the standing stones. The event lasted over thirty minutes and was followed by mysterious temperature fluctuations to as low as -10°C. Sudden drops of temperature are often reported with other types of ghostly phenomena, but rarely so low and almost never in the month of July. The Backstone circle was finally recognised by archaeologists and awaits excavation.

Not everyone is afraid of ghosts, that is until they see one. Walker Philip Saville was nearing Ilkley on a dark and damp afternoon in the 1930s when he had a memorable encounter. Having joined the road which skirts the eastern edges of the moor, Mr Saville came across a large black dog sitting in the middle of the road. As he walked towards the creature, snapping his fingers and attempting to entice the dog to him, a strange thing took place. In his words, 'The dog just disappeared. It neither walked away nor ran – it vanished.' The effect of this ghostly dog was instantaneous:

I shall never forget the terror which came over me. I went all over 'goose lumps'. I snatched my cap from off my head and ran (never slackening speed) until I got into Hawksworth village, where I almost ran into four ladies who were standing talking just round the corner by the graveyard. I don't know what I said but I felt I must talk – I was scared.

This experience could perhaps be rationalised as the imaginings of a bored or wandering mind were it not for the fact that others have come forward with similar stories of the ghost dog of the moor edges. Gytrash, as the hound is known locally, has been seen many times on that particular stretch of road, and farmers often warned ramblers to be on the look-out for the creature. Locals took Gytrash very seriously and regarded it as a type of boggard. In nearby Yeadon's Town Book there are actually records of sums of money being paid out for 'boggard catching'.

It should come as no surprise that such an expanse of wilderness as Ilkley Moor attracts strange characters to it or that the elemental nature of the place should lead to their developing superhuman powers of perception. The most famous of these moorland hermits was Wise Robin of Rombalds Moor. Renowned throughout the area as something of a wizard and latter-day shaman, Robin was held in awe by locals and frequently consulted on such topics as the weather, childbirth and the future generally. His speciality was lost or stolen goods and his prowess at seeing into the future in such matters was confirmed in 1790, when the Kendal Carrier was robbed near Keighley. The carrier's owners consulted Robin as to the consequences if the goods were not returned. He retired to the moor for silent communion with his muse and then returned with the statement, 'If the goods are not returned by Lady Day the thieves will be sorry.'

The goods failed to be returned and the local inhabitants, mindful of Robin's previous successes, prepared for the worst. Children, pets and livestock were kept indoors and all buildings secured. Weighted stones were even thrown over the roofs of some houses and farmsteads. On 25 March, Lady Day, a terrible storm ripped through the area, causing great damage. Whether or not the thieves were affected by it we are not told, but to the locals it was yet further proof of Wise Robin of Rombalds Moor's efficacy.

Finally, of all the mysteries which remain concerning Ikley Moor one offers the chance to discover a real physical treasure. A mixture of known history and legendary speculation tells of a sword once owned by Hacon, the foster son of King Athelstan, who had close connections with Bingley on the western side of the moor. This sword was one of many magical swords said to exist in those times and according to one chronicler of old Bingley, the blade was of such strength that Hacon 'was able to cleave a quern to the centre eye!' This sword was hidden on Ilkley Moor sometime in the Dark Ages and still awaits discovery by some lucky explorer.

The Yorkshire Dales

Of the Dales Halliwell Sutcliffe wrote, 'There's not a moor-road, or a field path, but is beset by its own haunting.' It is not just the roads and paths either, for the entire Dales area has a parallel world – a subterranean maze of caves, potholes and abandoned mines, all equally if not more haunted than the surface.

In his 1781 book *A Tour of the Caves*, the Revd John Hotten described the caves of Wharfedale as being 'the homes of giants, goblins and fairies', and for miners the workings beneath the moors at Greenhow above Pateley Bridge were home to every conceivable manifestation of subterranean horror. Something, perhaps the Earth Spirit herself, did not want the lead removed from the ground and miners had to fight both natural and supernatural forces for every gram of it.

When Greenhow miners found a colleague lying dead in a gallery with unnatural marks on his throat, they were unsympathetic as it was common knowledge that to work alone was to invite trouble from the trolls who roamed the empty chambers. A group of men killed in one mine collapse became bound to the shafts in which they perished and their spirits, known as the 'ghostly shift', warned others on more than one occasion to vacate the workings just before a roof-fall took place.

Later generations of miners came to the area from Cornwall and added their own pantheon of spirits to those already inhabiting the mines. Among these were the 'knockers', a noisy subterranean race of goblins whose mission was to aid miners by knocking loudly whenever the miners were nearing a rich seam or, confusingly, to warn of impending danger. Life was hard enough working long hours beneath the ground without the need to contend with duplicitous spirits.

To counteract these supernatural forces the miners took protective devices into the mines with them. Naturally-holed stones known as 'dobbie stones' were highly sought after, and if hung in the galleries or around the neck they were sure to offer protection against the workings of evil. Buildings on the surface were festooned with horseshoes, and trees such as the mountain ash (or rowan) were planted at mine heads to give protection against witchcraft. These talismans can be seen today in any village in the Dales, and many houses still have a water-worn dobbie stone outside or a rowan tree in the garden.

The Norse tradition gave Trollers Ghyll at Appletreewick its name, but the troll left the chasm a long time ago to be replaced by a ghost dog or barguest. The barguest was encountered one night by a travelling cobbler, who recalled that he looked 'as big as a littlish bear'. The ghost passed so close to his hiding place that the terrified man could see the creature was:

> . . . yellow, with great eyes like saucers. He'd a shaggy sort o' smell as he went by, and I counted myself for dead. But he chanced not to glimpse me, praise all the saints that ever were.

The barguest was more successful on other occasions. An Appletreewick man was found dead after traversing the gorge at night and an 1881 source records that marks were found 'impressed on the dead man's breast, but they seemed not by mortal hand'. Traveller Edmund Bogg recorded another foolhardy victim of Trollers Ghyll, John Lambert, who was proudly 'a sceptic

Trollers Ghyll at Appletreewick, haunt of a terrifying barguest

as far as the barguest was concerned'. Armed only with a stick he went after the creature, and was found dead the next morning.

Tales still told in the Dales carry with them the last vestiges of belief in the power of certain locations to heal the mind and body of almost any ill. Holy wells are still used in this way. Beneath Grassington Bridge at Threshfield there is a spring of fresh water called Our Lady's Well, the name being a Christianisation of a well formerly dedicated to the Earth Goddess. Its waters were famous for their curative properties and are still used to treat skin and eye complaints. The well was also used as a sanctuary from evil, and a Girston man took refuge here one night after being confronted with Pam the Fiddler, a notorious Threshfield ghost.

He stood in the holy water all night as the ghost stalked round him, waiting for him either to make a run for it or to lose strength. But the man, a tinker by trade, stuck it out until the ghost faded away with the dawn. Relieved, but certain he would die of exposure, he found that far from debilitating him, the night spent in the well's freezing water had completely rejuvenated him. Perhaps here we see a story, confused by time and retelling, of the efficacy of these locations to heal and protect against decay and evil.

Pam the Fiddler's ghost was eventually dealt with in an amusing but ultimately ineffectual manner. Her main haunt was the school at Threshfield, where the rector often wrote his sermons. One evening when he returned to retrieve some papers he had forgotten, Pam set upon him, resenting the intrusion into her lair. This was the final straw for the man of God and he hatched a most un-Christian plot to deal with her. He left an open bottle of brandy in the headmaster's study, returning later to find the ghost dead-drunk on the floor.

Swiftly he killed her and buried the body in the school grounds; an act he was to regret eternally as he should have known it is impossible to kill a ghost. Pam changed her affections from Threshfield to the rector and became his personal demon, following him wherever he went and haunting him until the end of his days.

At one time St Helen's Well near Threshfield was visited by pilgrims from all over the north and was an ornate affair, surrounded by a low retaining wall complete with carvings and an adjacent chapel for prayer and meditation. It is now ruined but is still an evocative place to visit and spend time at. Its ancient origins can still be found with patience – Guy Ragland Philips advises: 'Bend double beside the pool, and feel the big stones that stand under-water at the junctions of the kerbstones, and you will find that they are carved [Celtic] stone heads.'

Whatever rituals were once practised here are now lost to memory but survive in the local tradition of tying ribbons to the well bushes and casting pennies for wishes. There may have been a darker side to this well, as people still remember when it was considered reckless to walk past it on the evening of 24 June, the old date of Midsummer Day.

The Ebbing and Flowing Well at the side of the old A65 road out of Settle has its legend too. A naiad, another name for a wood spirit, fleeing to escape the unwanted attentions of another, more ardent sprite, begged for higher intervention to save her virtue. As she lay in the forest, camouflaged in the leaves but with her heart pounding in fear, she was transformed into a bubbling spring; all that remained of her previous existence was the beating of her heart reflected in the ebbing and flowing of the water.

The Ebbing and Flowing Well is featured in the Giggleswick church dedicated to St Alkeld, where a stained-glass window depicts sacrifices being made at the well. This is no simple legend either; in 1890 the water flow was carefully measured and was found to fill and empty every three and a half minutes or so. Sadly, quarrying work during the Second World War all but ruined the water pulse, but the well and its name remain.

North of Skipton there is an old lane between Cracoe and Rylestone church, running parallel to the B6265, which is home to a barguest. It is still remembered and when the author was investigating UFO sightings in the area in the early 1980s, local folk enquired if he was 'looking for the ghost dog – we still see it you know.'

Rylestone Fell has a long history of Will-o'-the-wisp sightings which in the middle years of this century turned into UFO reports. A strip of almost luminescent rock, which can be seen high on the fell, was mistaken by two policemen for a UFO hovering above the moors. This resulted in hundreds of UFO-spotters flocking to the area and a television appearance for the rock. Witnesses claimed they had seen the Cracoe UFO in the air, until it was revealed that the photographs depicted only a natural phenomenon.

These modern cases where natural phenomena have been proved to be the stimulus for ghost and UFO reports may give some

The Ebbing and Flowing Well near Settle

Stained-glass window at St Alkeld's Church, Giggleswick, depicting the Ebbing and Flowing Well

insight into the powers of the human mind to create mystery from everyday life. This in no way diminishes first-hand experience of these wonders, but can prevent us from sliding back into the superstitious practices of old.

A cave in Elbolton Hill was discovered years ago to contain prehistoric relics and bones, which at the time of discovery were thought to be the remains of fairies, adding to the traditions already strong in the area. Even the name of the hill is suggestive of the denizens of fairyland, being derived from 'elf bolt', the name given to the neolithic arrow heads once thought to belong to the fairies. This assumption may not be far from the truth if fairy stories are, as many theorists suggest, folk memories of the neolithic peoples who fled to the hills and caves when the Bronze Age folk became dominant in the British Isles.

Whatever their origin, the fairies lived on at Elbolton and wreaked their mischief on humans throughout the centuries. Daniel Waddilove was one mortal who fell prey to their enchantments while wandering on Elbolton Hill. For some reason he was in dispute with the fairy inhabitants and the fairy queen of the hill let the spirit Puck loose on him, with the result that Daniel was led astray all night, with Will-o'-the-wisp lights taking him from one bog to another.

Eventually, tiring of her sport the queen summoned Daniel and, offering her hands to be kissed, said, 'Mock us no more and go free.' Daniel was overawed and agreed. In telling the tale later he said of the fairy queen, 'She'd a voice like a lile, silver trumpet; and I wish I could hear it again.'

On the eastern side of Elbolton, near Thorpe, a doctor once encountered a tribe of fairies celebrating and he attempted to join them by breaking into their ring of enchantment. Once their dance was broken by mortal interference they reacted wildly, throwing the doctor around in the whirl, pinching and punching him before they fled. In the confusion he managed to catch a fairy, slipping it in his pocket, thinking that when he reached town this would be positive proof of their existence. But by the time he reached Cracoe and was ready to amaze the world with his find, the magic had trickled away and all he had in his pocket was dust.

Ralph Calvert, a shoemaker from Thorpe, had a chance meeting with the Prince of Darkness while walking back from Fountains Abbey where he had delivered shoes. In a gorge near Pateley

Bridge he encountered a casually dressed stranger who invited him to share a picnic. It was the Devil, in disguise and full of charm, until he finally revealed himself with a flourish and demanded the man's soul.

Ralph was unimpressed by this show and at first refused to believe him, suspecting his satanic majesty, due to the lack of the traditional horns and tail of 'being an effete southerner up to some stupid trick'. Ralph issued a challenge, saying he would only admit the stranger was the Devil if he demonstrated his powers by bridging the beck next to where they were eating. Sure enough, the beck had a bridge within three days – a rare case of the Devil being caught out by his own pride.

Despite intrusions by Scots raiders, Bolton Abbey was home to thousands of Augustinian monks between the twelfth and sixteenth centuries and, if we are to believe the accumulation of eye-witness testimonies, many of them never left, choosing to stay in the tranquil surroundings. Ghostly black-clad monks are frequently seen gliding through the grounds, usually on the path between the vicarage and the priory.

There was a spate of sightings earlier this century. The young Marquis of Hartington saw the transparent figure of a monk standing at his bedroom door while holidaying at the nearby rectory in

Bolton Abbey, haunt of Augustinian monks and mysterious forces

1912; and the ghost of Prior Moon, the last prior at Bolton Abbey before the dissolution of the monasteries by Henry VIII, is also bound to the ruins. His ghost has often been seen in the priory beneath a curious roof boss, described in Walbran's *Guide to Ripon* as being 'sagely conjectured by the country people to represent the devil'.

During excavations in 1973, archaeologists working on the tomb of John de Clifford were plagued by a series of hauntings and eerie experiences which they believed were connected with the 'curse of the Cliffords'.

In a *Yorkshire Post* article headed 'Curse Ends Tomb Search', members of the team revealed how they had felt and seen the ghost of an Augustine monk at the location given by Walbran. Others had seen ghosts in their homes, and one man fell ill after working on the tomb. He told archaeologist David Clough that, 'He was having no more to do with the tomb and said we could not use his tools. He had been ill with 'flu and believed his illness was due to the digging.' He went on to say, 'I have had the curse of the Cliffords on me this last week.' The man's wife also told Clough she had experienced a vision of something 'very black and evil' at the mouth of the tomb. Clough himself encountered a mysterious force in the priory, something so 'very strong and very frightening' that he had to leave the building before the feeling vanished.

Two miles upstream along the Wharfe valley is the Strid, a narrow gap in the rocks where the river is naturally compressed, boiling and seething as it forces itself down to the shallows at the priory. Some idea of the power involved here can be gained from the fact that the river is squeezed from a width of 15 to 1.5 metres wide in the space of only a couple of metres. Tradition says this is the site of the death of the 'Boy of Egremond' and many others have died here trying to jump to the other side, making the spot a fitting place for the ghostly White Horse of Wharefdale, which emerges from the swirling pool at times to warn the observer of a coming death.

Hobs were particularly common spirits in the Dales. The name 'hob' originates from Scandinavian settlers in the region and refers to a place spirit or *genus loci*. Hobs were usually disruptive but could occasionally be helpful, provided humans didn't meddle in their work. At Sturfit Hall near Reeth the resident hob was content to churn milk, attend to the fires and so forth until the mistress of the house left a new cloak and hat for him, in the mistaken belief he needed thanks for his work. The hob took one look and said, 'Ha! A cap and a hood, Hob'll never do mair good.' The hob which once dwelt at Close House Farm near Skipton was just as choosy. After years of faithful service he was given a new red hood in gratitude, and promptly downed tools and left the farm for good.

Hobs were also the guardians of moors and lonely stretches of road, and Hob Lanes can still be located in the Dales today, showing how the belief has lasted. One such hob was frequently seen on the road at Blea Moor, between Newby Head and Gearstones. He had the alarming habit of rushing out from the shadows, leaping on to a passing cart and riding for a while before disappearing again. Regular travellers on the road became used to him and he was affectionately known as 'Lile Hob'. Lile Hob seems in some way to have been watching over buried treasure, for when three Celtic arm bracelets were discovered on the moor near the Ribblehead Viaduct he ceased to appear.

These same moors also hold the spirits of an army of men dressed in ragged clothing, often seen descending from the Whernside fells into Dentdale. Up to a hundred of these ghosts at a time have been sighted and they are thought to be either phantoms of the bands of Vikings which invaded this area in the Dark Ages or, more likely, the ghostly remnants of the Scots 'moss troopers' which terrorised the north of England in the fourteenth century.

Ghosts are sometimes so persistent that they cannot be lived with, nor will exorcism remove them. In these cases it seems that some portion of a human soul has become not only earthbound but placebound, unable to leave one particular spot. One such case existed in Upper Wensleydale near Appersett, where Rigg House and Rigg Cottage were once one big house owned by a man called Metcalfe. His reputation in the area was poor as he had once been a slave trader, gaining the nickname 'Blackwhipper'. This reputation was further diminished when an elderly woman who lived with him vanished in mysterious circumstances, leading locals to suspect that Metcalfe was in some way responsible.

This rumour was strengthened with the frequent appearance of her ghost, which eventually and fittingly drove Metcalfe away from the place. However, subsequent owners and inhabitants were also troubled by her, so much so that in an effort to lay the ghost once and for all, the middle section of the mansion, where she had lived and now haunted, was demolished. This dramatic remedy must have been effective as the legend says that the ghost faded into memory as quickly as the missing part of the house.

Strange ceremonies, now seen simply as quaint folk traditions, linger on in these northern dales. Their origins are now totally unknown but are most likely connected with ancient rituals involving the cycle of the seasons, crop-planting times and boundary markings. The numerous fell races in the Dales may once have been annual boundary observances, and even the many May and autumn fairs and saints' day celebrations may well have their roots in an age when the year was split and marked by feasts and festivals which, if missed or ignored, invited the displeasure of long-forgotten gods and goddesses.

At the Wensleydale village of West Witton on the Saturday closest to 24 August, St Bartholomew's Day, a curious activity takes place. When darkness has fallen, an effigy similar to a bonfire 'guy' and named Bartle is ritually paraded round the village accompanied by almost all the villagers. The figure is destroyed and renewed every year except for the facial mask, which is stored with a local family traditionally responsible for the effigy's construction. Every now and then the procession halts at a particular house or spot in the village and this rhyme is chanted:

On Penhill Crags he tore his rags
At Hunters Thorn he blew his horn
At Capplebank Stee he brak his knee
At Grisgill Beck he brak his neck
At Wadhams End he could not fend
At Grisgill End we made his end
Shout, lads, shout!

The rhyme concludes with a rousing 'Hip, Hip, Hooray!' and on goes the procession to the next location.

This ceremony, known as the 'Burning of Bartle', is a remnant of a folk ritual carried out in the area for hundreds if not thousands of years, and is drawn deep from legendary sources. One account of the bizarre ceremony attributes it to folk memory of the chase and capture of a sixteenth-century sheep thief. But folklorist Ian Taylor believes it is the acting out of a far older legend concerning a giant who once lived on nearby Penhill, who was slain by a ghostly wolfhound after terrorising the village.

Women in black haunt the area too, and a ghostly black-clad lady has often been seen walking the route from the gates of Coverham church to a spot known as 'Courting Wall Corner' on Middleham Moor. This particular ghost was so feared that local inhabitants would be wary of crossing the moor alone at night. She was once seen by three ladies who were driving a horse and trap across the moor and, thinking the figure was flesh and blood, asked her to open a gate for them. At this request the apparition vanished leaving the terrified women to ride home in silence.

Her haunting, like so many others of the 'grey' or 'black' lady type, was claimed to be the result of a love triangle that went wrong, ending in a murder. The story may even have some basis in fact, as sometime in the 1940s the body of a woman was discovered by peat-cutters on the moor. Her clothes, what was left of them, were black.

Coverdale now has a phantom light, seen on the A684 road between the hamlets of Caldbergh and West Scrafton. The spook-light appears to motorists as though a car were coming towards them down the narrow country lanes and naturally they slow down to await its passing. Most are shocked that after a long wait no car passes them, the light merely remaining stationary until it vanishes. If the driver ignores the other 'car' and drives straight towards it, the light simply disappears.

The 'Pennine Light', as it is known, is most commonly seen in the long winter nights and legend connects this vehicular Will-o'-the-wisp with the ruins of St Simon's Chapel, situated in the fields near where the light appears. Chantry Farm nearby is also the haunt of a 'grey lady' ghost which seems to be bound in some way to the staircase, where it is most often seen and more frequently heard.

Fifteenth-century Nappa Hall at Askrigg is yet another stately home allegedly haunted by Mary Queen of Scots. She was once allowed to visit her friend Sir Christopher Metcalf here during her time of incarceration at Bolton Castle, and so liked the hospitality that she returned as a ghost following her execution.

One account of this royal haunting speaks of her being seen by two children playing hide-and-seek. One of the girls saw the apparition and chased it, believing it to be one of the maids, and was just reaching out to touch the dress when:

. . . she turned round and I saw her face. It was very lovely. Her

Beneath Richmond Castle there is reputedly a secret chamber, where King Arthur and his knights are held in timeless enchantment

dress seemed to be made of black velvet. After looking at me for a moment she went on, and disappeared through the door leading to the winding stone staircase in the angle turret of the west tower.

Swaledale is haunted by a headless black dog at the humpbacked bridge near Ivelet, but it is Richmond Castle at the head of the dale which has the most interesting legend.

In a secret stone chamber somewhere beneath the castle keep is said to lie a table on which there is a large sword and a hunting horn. Anyone finding these items and following the correct sequence of drawing the sword from its scabbard and blowing the horn can expect a shock. For these actions will rouse King Arthur and his knights who are held here in a timeless subterranean enchantment.

In the distant past this chamber was discovered by Potter Thompson when he was searching for lost sheep. Foolishly, instead of using the sword and horn to rouse the knights, he was more interested in the fabulous treasure which lay scattered about them, and as he reached out to grab some of it a sonorous voice spoke:

Potter Thompson, Potter Thompson,
If thou hadst either drawn
The sword or blown the horn,
Thou'dst have been the luckiest man
That ever yet was born!

The voice so terrified the shepherd that he shot out of the cavern which immediately closed behind him.

- Semer Water can be an eerie and atmospheric place on the brightest of days, and it is probably this isolated, wild quality which has amplified and developed the strange tales surrounding it. One of writer Jessica Lofthouse's aunts recounted a story to her of a long night's lonely watch at Raydale House in the vicinity. As she settled herself to a night of nursing an invalid the aunt heard the sound of a horse galloping up to the hall, a rider dismounting and a banging on the door. When the door was opened there was no one to be seen, nor were there any hoof-prints in the mud.

A sunken village is supposed to lie beneath the surface of Semer Water, drowned in a catastrophe brought about by the village's refusal to help an outsider. In some versions of the story the outsider is an angel, in others a witch. In both cases the visitor had travelled to the area to test the manners of the people there, who were legendary for their selfishness and greed.

The visitor asked for sanctuary at the gates as night and bad weather drew in and was harshly refused, being driven from the town. He went instead to a small cottage on the hillside where a peasant family lived. Here he was invited in and treated with great hospitality despite the family's own lack of resources. He woke the next morning and stood on the fell high above the town of Semerwater chanting the following spell:

Semerwater rise, and Semerwater sink,
And drown all the town but one little house
Where they gave me meat and drink.

At this the water rose and engulfed the town leaving only the cottage on the hillside. Over the years people have claimed to hear the old church bells ringing under the water and occasionally someone will report seeing buildings at the bottom of the lake. There was probably once a prehistoric village at the side of the lake or on an artificial island here, which gave way to a folk memory and subsequent legend. The Carlow Stones on the lakeside are alleged to be all that remain of the lost settlement and they too have mystery attached, rumoured to be the site of a druid altar thrown there by the Devil from the top of Addleborough Hill during a contest of strength.

The summit of Addleborough has stories of buried treasure, secreted there by a giant who was carrying it between Skipton and Pendragon Castle further north. The treasure, a chest containing gold and jewels, is buried underneath the cairn of Stone Raise and guarded by a fairy watchman. A 'devil's stone' or natural boulder also on Addleborough's flat top suggests that this hill, together with Penhill (with its giant), may have been an old 'holy hill' in times gone by.

Buried treasure left by retreating Celtic tribesmen might also be found by the daring on the Swaledale hill of Harkeside. The legend and lure of this gold – the Celts were famous for their finely wrought gold jewellery – have led quite a few to seek it out. All attempts were doomed to failure and Jessica Lofthouse sums up the perils of looking for treasure buried for religious reasons in this dramatic account of one futile expedition:

Seekers with picks and spades worked hard but the guardians, giant birds with flapping wings, beat them back, smashing their lanterns. One gang made three fruitless break-ins, the last attempt coinciding with thunderstorm and cloudburst, as though all the underworld demons were against them.

According to legend, buried treasure lies at Harkeside in Swaledale

York

York has been called the 'city of a thousand ghosts' and the supernatural is so popular here that three 'ghost tours' are run to satisfy visitors' demands for the eerie. Because of its 2,000-year continuous inhabitation by several different races and cultures, the city has accrued a wealth of traditions, legends and customs.

York Minster stands on a site of great religious antiquity. Legends tell of how King Edwin forsook paganism at the major pagan temple of Goodmanham to the east, and gave St Paulinus a site formerly occupied by Roman barracks on which to found a church. The key point here is that the site was also that of a holy well, now known as St Cuthbert's Well, which was venerated as home of the earth force for thousands of years before either Romans or Vikings came to the region. In the tradition of Christianisation of pagan sites, the present-day Minster was founded on 12 April 627. The well in which King Edwin was baptised can still be seen in the crypt of the Minster, the location adding weight to the legend, as this is the oldest part of the structure.

There are a number of saints' miracles connected with the Minster. One concerns St William, who in 1141 became Archbishop of York. His tenure was stormy and he was deposed on one occasion by Pope Eugenius before being reinstated and subsequently canonised in the thirteenth century.

His canonisation came about as a result of the thirty-six miracles he performed during his life, of which the most famous took place on his home-coming after being deposed. As he returned to the city, welcoming crowds thronged the streets and the dilapidated wooden bridge over the River Ouse was so weighed down that the structure collapsed, depositing hundreds of celebrants into the river. William averted certain tragedy by making the sign of the cross and offering a prayer for help. The waters of the Ouse instantly moulded themselves into a bridge over which the drowning people could escape to safety. This and other miracles performed by the saint can be seen portrayed in some excellent stained-glass work in St William's window in the north transept of the Minster.

Historic York Minster has witnessed many mysterious happenings

One of the many ghost stories attributed to the Minster concerns a group of people who were viewing the building one summer's evening in the 1920s, when two of the party, Mr G. and Ms C., became separated from the others. As they stood admiring the architecture they noticed a man standing near them dressed in full naval uniform, who appeared to be staring intently at Ms C. As Mr G. looked from the man to his companion he saw that she was white with terror, her lips drawn tight, obviously gripped with emotion, staring at the naval officer. Mr G. turned back to the intruder who walked across to the pair, leaned over to mutter something in Ms C.'s ear, and walked on. Astonished at the encounter, which had no obvious explanation, Mr G. attempted to catch up with the retreating man but he vanished among the evening strollers outside. When Mr G. returned, Ms C. had regained her composure and was trying to account to the rest of the party for what had taken place. Like many people she was interested in the possibility of survival after death, and she related how she had made a pact with her brother, with whom she was very close, to the effect that whoever died first would appear to the other if an afterlife made it possible.

Her brother had subsequently joined the Royal Navy and she had forgotten about the agreement until now, when she had seen him in the Minster. Despite assurances from her companions that she must have been mistaken, Ms C. insisted that the man had been her brother and the words he whispered in her ear were, 'There is a future state.' The woman's account of the experience went on:

The instant it uttered those words my fears were confirmed; I knew my poor brother was dead and that what I looked at was only his ghost or shadow.

The family was officially informed a few weeks later of the man's death, and the time and date given in the official communiqué were determined to be exactly those of the experience in the Minster.

York Minster has been ravaged by fire at least four times in its existence, leading one guidebook to describe the destroying force as a 'fire demon'. An apt phrase, considering the legends which have sprung up to account for the destruction of the south transept by fire on the night of 8 July 1984. The official explanation for the fire was lightning, but many people refused to believe that a building so well protected against the elements could be immolated so swiftly, and weathermen added to the mystery when they claimed that although there had been a few thunderstorms in the region, none were known to have occurred within ten miles of the Minster.

The ensuing legends were split equally between those who favoured a religious element involving the wrath of God and those who preferred the idea of alien intervention.

Just two days previously the Rt Revd David Jenkins had been installed as Bishop of Durham, causing considerable rancour within the Church due to his interpretation of Jesus' miracles as stunts and misinterpretations, and his reference to the Resurrection in one newspaper as 'a conjuring trick with bones'. When the blaze struck the Minster many of Jenkins' opponents claimed this was direct intervention from God, who was showing his disgust at the heretic's statements.

The popular newspapers took up the story with headlines such as: 'An Act of God?' (*Daily Star*) and 'The Wrath of God' (*Sun*). When questioned as to his belief about the fire's origins, purpose and meaning, the Revd Mowll told the *Sun*, 'I'm not surprised people are talking about divine intervention.'

If the claim of divine destruction was bizarre then the other major legendary explanation for the inferno was even stranger. The 'fire demon' in this case was claimed to be a UFO. On the night of the fire several people saw an orange UFO hovering above the Minster, including taxi driver Bill Whitehead, who reported seeing a glowing orb shooting orange flame down on to the roof of the building, and Eddie Acaster who observed a cigar-shaped object above the Minster. Of course, neither claim can ever be proved and the rationalists eventually settled for the safe explanation that the mystery fire was caused by 'side flash' from a malfunctioning lightning conductor.

York is no stranger to unexplained aerial phenomena. In the year 1199 'something' descended from the sky and was recorded by the religious chronicler, Abbot Ralph. He wrote:

In the time of King Richard I of England, there appeared in a certain grassy, flat ground, human footprints of extraordinary length; and everywhere the footprints were impressed, the grass remained as if scorched by fire.

This took place sometime in the decade between 1189 and 1199.

The Treasurer's House in York is widely famed for its collection of period furniture, and although the present building is mainly sixteenth- and seventeenth-century, the site has been occupied since at least Roman times, evidence of which exists in the shape of a Roman column in the cellar. In his book *This Haunted Isle*, Peter Underwood relates the story of a troop of Roman soldiers, seen there during the 1950s. The soldiers burst through the walls of a cellar to the sound of a trumpet, startling an apprentice plumber who was working there.

The ghosts were a raggle-taggle bunch led by a horseman, and from the description given by the witness, looked as if they were returning in defeat from a battle. The curious feature of the sighting is that the figures had no legs visible below knee-height. This seemingly insignificant observation became relevant when it was learned that the level of the old Roman road was below that of the cellar; meaning the ghosts were actually marching at the level of their own time period – possibly shocked at seeing what was to them the ghost of a twentieth-century plumber hovering in the air some 30 centimetres above the road.

The soldiers marched straight across the cellar and disappeared through another wall. Before the terrified plumber had time to blurt out his story to the Treasurer's House curator, he was asked, 'You've seen the Romans, haven't you?' His sighting is corroborated by the present-day curator who holds statements from other witnesses of the ghostly legion.

The religious presence in the city has led to the appearance of ghosts in a number of sacred buildings. The Church of the Holy Trinity which stands in Micklegate is haunted by the abbess of a convent once belonging to the church. She was killed by soldiers during the dissolution of the monasteries when she refused to leave the convent, telling the troops that they would enter the nunnery only when she was dead, and if they slew her she would return to haunt the spot until the ground was reconsecrated.

Even though Holy Trinity Church was subsequently erected there her ghost became bound to the site and was repeatedly seen by church-goers. A letter in the 6 May 1876 edition of the *Ripon and Richmond Chronicle* gives an account of one experience:

In the middle of the service, my eyes, which had hardly once moved from the left or north side of the window, were attracted by a bright light, formed like a female, robed and hooded, passing from north to south, with a rapid gliding motion . . . The robe was long and trailed. About half an hour later, it again passed from north to south, and having remained about ten seconds only, returned with what I believe to have been the figure of a small child . . .

The figure was seen many times and always through the same windows, leading to suspicion that it was an illusion created by tree branches blowing in the wind. In an attempt to lay the ghost one rector had the trees cut down, confident this would end the sightings, and for a while nothing was seen. The rational clergyman congratulated himself on his ability to banish superstition. But then, several months later, the figure was seen again flitting past the window during a marriage ceremony.

Ghostly organ music has been heard in the depths of night emitting from the Theatre Royal in St Leonard's Place. The old building is also home to the ghosts of a nun and of an actor who died during a duel and returned to haunt his favourite theatre. In a vain effort to recapture the success of his acting days, the thespian has often been seen standing backstage or in the wings observing the performances.

The nun's origins are less easy to explain, although it is said that she worked at St Leonard's Hospital, which once occupied the site of the theatre. In a tragic story familiar to ghost-hunters everywhere, the nun was supposedly walled up alive in the Middle Ages for an unknown transgression of her vows.

The Museum library in York suddenly found itself at the centre of attention from the national press when a ghost was seen in the curator's office by caretaker George Jonas one evening in September 1953.

In an encounter lasting several minutes the caretaker watched the man stand up, walk past him with no acknowledgement and enter the library muttering, 'I must find it. I must find it.' Although it was late and no members of the public should have been in the building, the caretaker presumed that this was just an absent-minded scholar who had forgotten the time. He followed him into the library and was just about to ask if he could be of assistance when the figure faded away.

As it vanished the ghost dropped a book on the floor and,

perhaps wisely, the stunned caretaker left it where it lay so he could check the next day that he had not imagined the entire scene. Sure enough when he returned in the company of the curator the book was where the apparition had left it.

One month later the haunting was repeated at exactly the same time, 7.40pm, and this happened again on the following month. Both events were witnessed by Mr Jonas and (on one occasion) by an ex-soldier, when they both saw the same book, *Antiquities and Curiosities of the Church* by William Andrews, thud to the floor.

In an attempt both to prove the ghost's existence and his own sanity, Mr Jonas arranged an audience for the expected December visit of the ghost. Altogether six people, including a doctor and journalist, sat waiting. On this occasion the ghost was two minutes late, but at 7.42pm all present saw and heard the usual book being slid from the shelf and dropped to the floor, although no apparition was seen. The assembled sceptics were convinced they had been witness to a genuine supernatural event, and further investigation suggested that the apparition was of one Alderman Edward Wooler, a solicitor and antiquary from Darlington, who had formerly owned the book.

York's ghost trail can be also be followed through the public houses and inns of the city. Each floor of the Anglers Arms in Goodramgate has an unearthly presence. The top floor is home to a ghost smell, an odour of lavender which intermittently drifts through the rooms, while the first floor is alleged to be the haunt of a young child, thought to be dressed in late Victorian garb. The cellar of the pub holds a nameless horror which in the past has interfered with the beer-pumping mechanisms. Ghost-investigator Terence Whitaker was told that the subterranean entity was 'a creature of great age and intelligence and surrounded by utter evil'.

Legendary highwayman Dick Turpin was hanged at York in 1739 and his tomb can be seen in the churchyard of St Denys and St George. Turpin was a true folk hero and attained even more fame during his period of imprisonment. One newspaper account claimed that 'the whole country have flocked to see him and have been very liberal to him, inasmuch as he had wine constantly before him'. His jailers soon realised that money could be made from infamy and made over £100 by selling alcoholic beverages to Turpin and his admirers. Brave to the last, Turpin went to the gallows without complaint and even presented the attending chaplain with an ivory whistle to show there were no ill-feelings. Although as Britain's most famous highwayman Turpin is credited with the feat of riding from London to York in fifteen and half hours, it was actually another highwayman, Ben Nevison, who did it. He was also tried and hung at York, in 1685.

Being a major centre for legal matters with courts of all kinds regularly convening there, York was the main location in Yorkshire for trying witches during the seventeenth century. One of the ill-starred Pendle Witches, Jenny Preston from Gisburn, was tried, sentenced and executed at York, and one of Yorkshire's few witch-burnings took place in York in 1648. The 'wise woman' was alleged to have crucified her mother and sacrificed a small calf and a cockerel to Satan.

It is difficult in these cases to know just how much evidence was concocted by malicious witnesses and how much was actually belief and practice on the part of the witch. If these women really did believe they held such powers, it must have been a very strong belief indeed to risk the certain and horrific consequences if they were discovered. Nonetheless a relic of York's witchcraft days can be seen in the crypt of the Minster where there is a stone carving of a witch and her demon-like familiar (personal spirit guardian).

The outskirts of York have their own kind of ghosts. One in particular, known as 'Owd Nance', has been seen regularly over the years. Nance lived at Sherrif Hutton and was engaged to Tom, a long-distance mailcoach driver. However, during his enforced periods of absence she became besotted with a highwayman, whose child she bore. This dangerous liaison was discovered by Tom and the couple parted in acrimony, vowing never to see each other again.

Some years later as he neared York the coach driver came across the crying figure of Nance, child in arms, at the side of the road. Forgetting their previous differences he lifted them aboard the coach and drove quickly into York for assistance. As they travelled Nance sobbed out her story. She had been treated badly by the highwayman who eventually had gone back to his wife when the child was born, leaving them homeless and poverty-stricken. The coach drove hard to reach York and arrived at the Black Swan inn, formerly in Coney Street, but both Nance and the child died during the night. Before she passed away Nance promised Tom, 'If my spirit is allowed to return, I will always warn you, your childer, and your childer's childer of any coming danger.'

The coachman was devastated by her death but thought no more of the death-bed promise. However, Nance was true to her word. Years later, as he was driving past York through a thick and dangerous mist on what is now the A64, the ghost of Nance appeared beside him urging the horses to a gallop until they came to rest in the courtyard of the old Black Swan, whereupon the ghost faded away.

She returned on many subsequent occasions to help Tom out of trouble on the road and he passed on the knowledge to his son, who followed in his footsteps as a coachman. Since then the spirit of Owd Nance has been frequently seen on the A64, motorists reporting a ghostly white shape which appears in thick fog, warning of danger ahead, vanishing if any driver attempts to speak to her.

A battle also left its ghostly memory near York. On 2 July 1644, during the English Civil War, the Puritans led by Oliver Cromwell defeated the Royalist forces at Long Marston. Cromwell used the Old Hall at Long Marston village as his base for the battle and his ghost has reputedly been seen there on several occasions, pacing

Ghostly combatants roam the area around Marston Moor, scene of the famous Civil War battle in 1644

73

up and down, deep in thought before the conflict. Rumours of ghostly combatants seen in the area were rife for some years, and the rumour was confirmed in November 1932 when two motorists, lost while searching for the Wetherby road, came across a group of ragged-clothed men trudging alongside the road in the ditch.

As the motorists slowed down to ask if help was needed, they realised with a shock that the men were wearing clothes of the Cavalier fashion and appeared not to notice the twentieth-century travellers or their car. The Cavaliers clambered out of the ditch and wandered into the centre of the road, where they were run down by a bus travelling in the opposite direction. The car-drivers stopped and searched the area for what they were sure must be the bodies of the men but they found nothing. It seems they had witnessed a group of Royalists fleeing to safety from the defeat at Marston Moor.

Ghosts were seen on the edges of the city at Stockton-on-the-Forest in 1812, when two farmers saw a spectral army apparently on manoeuvres high above them. J. Horsfall Turner wrote of the event in 1888:

When looking after the cattle they were suddenly surprised to see at some distance what appeared to them a large body of armed men, in white military uniforms, in the centre of which was a person of commanding aspect in scarlet. After performing various aerial evolutions the whole body began to move in perfect order towards the summit of a hill, passing the spectators at the distance of about one hundred yards.

As the men watched, the ghostly column was joined by another troop of ghost soldiers, this time dressed in dark clothing, marching up the opposite side of the hill. The two forces met in the air on the hilltop and merged together as they disappeared down the far side of the hill. A thick curtain of smoke covered the plain with their passing and Turner noted: 'The time for the first appearance of this strange phenomenon to the clearing up of the smoke was no more than five minutes.' This could possibly have been a misperceived meteorological or astronomical phenomenon, but over a hundred years have now passed without a convincing explanation for the sight being put forward.

North Yorkshire and the Moors

From York the road towards the North Yorkshire Moors passes an airfield at Linton-on-Ouse. Once used as a base for Halifax bombers during the Second World War, it is now home to an RAF training squadron – and a ghost. Airman Walter Hodgson began to haunt the airfield in 1959 after his family had erected a plaque to his memory on the control tower. Since then, terrified air traffic controllers at the airfield have seen the ghost of a tall figure dressed in flying kit wandering the airfield. Sightings reached a peak during 1988, and the RAF were concerned enough to give a press conference at which they officially confirmed the haunting. One of the air traffic staff who saw the apparition said, 'It was a man about six feet tall. It moved towards the approach room and then disappeared. I was in hysterics.'

Travellers on the busy A1 trunk road to the west may catch a glimpse of three gigantic stones in a field near the market town of Boroughbridge. Standing up to 6 metres tall, they date from around 1700 BC and are among the largest standing stones in England.

Flasius, the ghost of a Roman centurion who died defending the fort at Aldborough, has been seen wandering the A1 here, having chosen to stay and guard the road where the legions marched. They too would have wondered at the origins of the mysterious monoliths known as the Devil's Arrows. In a dispute with the town of Aldborough the Devil was said to have thrown the standing stones from the top of How Hill, near Fountains Abbey, while shouting:

Borobrigg, keep out o' t'way
For Auldboro' town
I will ding down.

Camden notes that there were four arrows until 1532, when 'one was lately pulled down by someone who hoped in vain to find treasure'. No treasure was discovered and the felled stone was later used as a foundation stone in a bridge over the Test, a tributary of the River Ure.

An unexpected pagan 'green man' carving can be found in the abbey's Lady Chapel

Fountains Abbey near Ripon, a focal point for strange phenomena

Fountains Abbey near Ripon was once a thriving religious centre run by the Cistercian order of monks. The ruins, set in a spectacular natural amphitheatre, are all that is now left of the once wealthy abbey. Although no visible ghosts have been seen there, several visitors have reported hearing the eerie sound of monks chanting in the Cloister Court.

Robin Hood visited the abbey, giving his name to Robin Hood's Well, which is the site recorded in the ballads near which Robin fought the Curtal Friar, later to be Friar Tuck. For those who see Robin as a representation of the pagan gods, either in flesh or myth, the legend of him fighting with a man of the cloth is significant. The battle between pagan and Christian ended when they both fell in the river, becoming firm friends afterwards, perhaps a kind of baptism for the man of the woods.

A tradition that Robin's bow and arrows were once kept at the abbey has aroused much speculation, and people often wonder what became of these artefacts. In fact they never existed, yet can still be found there. They were not real weapons but carvings of a bow and arrow, still to be seen in the Lady Chapel.

A remnant of the vegetation spirit can still be seen by the curious at Fountains Abbey. On the inward wall of the Lady Chapel is an angel, as befits such a sacred building, but on the outer wall at the key stone of the window arch is a carving of a very different kind. Looking outward into wild nature is a stark 'green man' carving with snake-like vegetation issuing from its mouth. Once seen this carving is never forgotten and it is a testament to the underlying beliefs of even the builders of Christian edifices.

This part of Yorkshire seems to be a focal point for all types of strange phenomena, for just a few miles away at Thirsk there is Pudding Pie Hill, an ancient tumulus or burial mound, which is the dwelling place of a fairy tribe, and, in the 1960s, a ghost was photographed at Newby church. It has become one of the most convincing ghost photographs yet.

Oddly enough it was a member of the clergy who managed to snap the ghost while photographing the altar at Newby church near Ripon. Revd Lord did not see anything through the viewfinder at the time, and had no idea that his prints would come back from the chemist displaying a hooded and staring transparent figure standing just to the right of the altar.

Stranger still, the church had no history of a haunting and had only been built in 1870. The photograph and negative were thoroughly checked by experts and no evidence of fraud or film fault came to light. From the photograph and reference points in the church it was possible to estimate that the startling apparition was up to 2.7 metres tall.

A huge ghostly figure was photographed by the altar of Newby church in the 1960s

Crossroads are traditionally haunted locations. Witches were often buried there, as they could not be buried in consecrated ground and it was thought the cross formed by the roads would contain their spirit. The same rule applied to murderers who were once executed and hung in chains on a gibbet. The crossroads near Kirkby Wiske was the site of just such a gibbet, marked now by the Busby Stoop inn.

The pub gets its name from Thomas Busby, who murdered a local vagabond when a business deal went wrong. He was summarily tried and executed, and his body was brought back to hang at the crossroads. A contemporary account of the event can be found in the diaries of Leeds antiquarian Ralph Thoresby, who in May 1703 wrote: 'Along the banks of the Swale are the very pleasant gardens of Sir William Robinson, but a few miles further, a more doleful object of Thomas Busby hanging in chains is seen.'

Travellers passing that way alone on moonless nights are advised to keep their eyes firmly on the road as they near the crossroads, lest they should see the ghostly shadow of Busby swinging from the vanished gibbet. His spirit can also be seen looking out from one of the upstairs rooms of the Busby Stoop inn which faces the former gibbet site. Tradition states that anyone seeing either of these two apparitions will meet with misfortune before the next full moon.

Gabriel ratchets were often seen flying over North Yorkshire. Sceptics and those without the gift to see between the worlds would claim that they were merely flocks of wild geese, whose calls in the darkness sounded unearthly but were nevertheless harmless. The country folk of North Yorkshire knew otherwise, and to them the hounds were portents of death and destruction. Even the educated classes held a belief in this Norse legend.

David Naitby, the schoolmaster at Bedale, was no exception and in his diary for 11 October 1773 wrote: 'There is now a certainty of death to come among us. For the third time the ratchet pack hath hunted for souls over Bedale.' When no ill-luck followed his sighting of the Wild Hunt he still believed something was to happen and wrote on 18 October: 'But seven nights now gone since Gabriels raced overhead, and now there has come to us a blood red moon, a sure sign we are to be judged for our sins.'

Sutton Bank, the road which runs between Gormire and the Kilburn Horse up on to the moors, has a ghost light – a flickering spectre which travels up and down the A170 road at night. An old man who lived alone on the bank related one story concerning this spooklight to writer William Foggitt, in which he saw the light while out walking his dog. At first it was just a bright light, but as he watched and bravely crossed the road for a better view, the light formed into the shape of a thin young girl. As the ghostly waif passed the man, he felt a wave of icy air and the ghost vanished.

This story has a sequel. In 1936 the skeleton of a Bronze Age woman was discovered on Sutton Bank, exactly opposite the old man's house and the location of the ghost sighting. Since then the light has been seen but it never takes the form of the girl. The grave site is marked by an inscription.

Once the high plateau of the moors is reached the scenery changes dramatically. Moorland extends as far as the eye can see, broken only by the occasional road. Anyone crossing the moors, either by road or by one of the many footpaths, cannot help noticing the numerous burial mounds and standing stones which dot the moor. This area must once have been an important site of worship for prehistoric man, and the profusion of these monuments and megaliths creates a ritual landscape about which we can sadly now only speculate.

As Christianity came to the remote moorland hamlets and farms, the old standing stones and burial places were attributed to the Devil or to fairy origins, and preaching crosses began to spring up in their place. Some were undoubtedly modified pagan standing stones, others were simply set up on existing pagan sites, but just as the prehistoric stones and mounds attracted tales and legends, so did many of the numerous moorland crosses.

The crosses known as Old and Young Ralph and Fat Betty standing near the road at Rosedale Head are the most mysterious. In the Yorkshire tradition that stones are often named after people who have died at the mercy of nature, the tales attached to these stones developed from the legend of a boundary dispute involving Old Ralph, a Rosedale dweller, and the Prioress of Rosedale Abbey.

One legend tells that Ralph and the prioress were killed in bad weather while on the moors arguing about whose land was whose. The crosses and stones were erected to mark both their passing and the revised limits of Rosedale Abbey; boundary stones of a geographical area and also marking the boundary between life and death. The cross named Fat Betty is not actually a cross but a white painted rock repainted each year, and one of three stones in Yorkshire which are ritually treated in this way – a possible link with earlier stone veneration. Fat Betty and the other Rosedale crosses have all been used over the years by travellers to give offerings to the gods in the form of coins, which are still to be found in the cracks and fissures of the stones. If you find one only take it if you are really in need otherwise bad luck will follow.

At Fairy Cross Plain above Fryup, fairies were seen in the area at the beginning of this century. One farmer's wife saw a green-clad fairy many times over the years, and she would watch him and his friends come down from the moors and disappear into the ground by a stream bridge. When her sceptical husband expressed surprise at his wife's dealings with dwellers from the otherworld she casually pointed out to him that moles live undergound so why shouldn't fairies?

This deep-rooted faith in denizens of another world existing parallel with our own led to numerous superstitions, and up until very recently people on the moors were easy prey to belief in witches. Veterinary practice and agricultural knowledge was still in its infancy and any problems with either cattle or crops were attributed to the machinations of witchcraft. To counter this, 'cunning' or 'wise' men sprang up everywhere.

Whitby folklore researcher Edna Whelan is of the opinion that the last wise man of the moors died long ago. She was told that the sorcerer, Charlie Brocket, who lived at Ellers Cottage in Goathland, died sometime in the 1930s after a long life in which he enjoyed a good reputation for producing talismans and amulets to counteract the effects of witchcraft. After his death a bottle full of pins and needles, a well-known charm against spells, was discovered concealed in the chimney breast of his house.

Deep in Arncliffe Wood at Glaisdale is the Wishing Stone, a natural boulder surmounted by a tree. It was thought lucky to walk round it nine times while holding a wish in your mind. Writer Peter Walker, who was raised in Glaisdale, remembers doing this as a child and also placing coins in fissures in the rock or in a hollow in the tree. He also remembers searching fruitlessly for the legendary Robin Hood's Cave, thought to be in the woods. The cave was said to lead to a tunnel which in turn ran far under the moors to Robin Hood's Bay, and was used by the wandering outlaw to outwit his would-be captors and also for smuggling activities.

Travellers on the moorland road from Pickering to Whitby cannot fail to notice the Hole of Horcum, a huge depression scooped from the ground to the west of the road as it crosses Lockton Low Moor. It has become such a popular landmark that a car park now exists for motorists to view the scenery and the Devil's handiwork.

Local legend claims that the Devil scooped out the hollow with one hand and threw the spoil to the east where it landed to form the hill known as Blakey Topping. Other legends connected with the Hole of Horcum tell that the debris was thrown either north to form Freeborough Hill, under which King Arthur and his knights are said to sleep, or north-west to become Roseberry Topping.

Old Nick also gave his name to the Devil's Elbow, a sharp bend in the road to the north of the Hole. Nearby stands the Saltersgate Inn which claims to have a peat fire that has burned solidly at least since 1800. The origins of this perpetual flame appear to be yet another vestige of the agricultural year's rituals of carrying the light of the sun, in the form of a flame, from one year to the next.

When the Devil dropped in at the Saltersgate to seek shelter and food one dark and stormy night, he had not reckoned on meeting a local priest who was staying there. Naturally a dispute ensued and the priest performed an exorcism to banish the power of evil, whereupon the Devil slunk off to the kitchen but would not leave the inn. Realising the futility of this new-fangled Christianity, the local people employed a far older method and immediately lit a peat fire which trapped the Devil in the smoke. Tradition says he cannot perform evil in the pub as long as the fire is kept burning in

Saltersgate Inn, site of a perpetual flame

81

Dalby Maze in the Howardian Hills, site of an old maze-running tradition

some part of the building, and it now smoulders happily in the public bar. This story is so well-known that the inn had its sign changed to read 'The Legendary Saltersgate Inn'.

One of Britain's many enigmatic mazes stands by the roadside at Dalby, in the Howardian Hills just off the B1363. This is one of the few mazes cut from turf and Yorkshire's only existing example. Despite extensive studies no one really knows the purpose of these mazes, whose history can be traced back to the ancient Greeks. Consequently they attract legends and tradition. One of these involves the running of the maze, and the labyrinth at Dalby, also known as the 'City of Troy', has a local tradition warning that no one should run the maze more than the magical number of nine times or bad luck will befall them.

There was also a maze at Asenby near Thirsk, behind the Shoulder of Mutton public house. This maze, long since vanished, was carved into an ancient earthwork known as Fairy Hill. As recently as 1908 local people would perform the traditional maze-running and the antiquarian Hadrian Allcroft recorded that some villagers could remember 'treading it on many a summer's evening and kneeling down at the centre to hear the fairies singing'.

St Mary's Church at Lastingham was originally founded by St Cedd as a monastery, and according to the Venerable Bede in AD 731, St Cedd was aware of an ancient power there and 'wished to purify the site of the monastery from the taint of earlier crimes by prayer and fasting'. This took the entire period of Lent, after which a monastery, later superseded by the church, was built.

The crypt at Lastingham in the oldest part of the church still harbours a strange and tangible atmosphere. As the church guide says: 'If you walk down the stairs to the crypt you are stepping back in time. In this holy place the spirits of Cedd and Chad move on the stones of the floor and in the air you breathe.'

Scattered about in this subterranean chamber, unchanged for over a thousand years, are several Anglo-Saxon carvings with their interlocking designs. There is also a dragon stone dating from the eighth century, thought to have once been part of the abbot's throne.

Whether it is a combination of these strange stones and imagination or whether some ancient power still flows at Lastingham is uncertain, but several people have had strange experiences in the crypt, including the normally sceptical author, who had to leave rapidly on one occasion due to what can only be described as a 'supernatural pressure' in the air.

When author Guy Ragland Philips took a witch to the church, her natural sensitivity felt an evil influence emanating from the eastern end of the crypt. While in the crypt she 'dowsed' several

The atmospheric crypt at Lastingham church

stones there, pronouncing each one all right until she came to the remains of the Ana Cross which had been brought down from the moors years before. As she touched it she found the source of the power, and said, 'This is it. It's horrible – very evil. It sticks to my hand.'

The church is haunted too. One of its previous incumbents, Canon Gordon Thompson, claimed that he had encountered a disembodied spirit several times near the door between the vestry and the sanctuary.

Pubs seem to have an attraction for ghosts of all types. Whether this is to do with the human dramas played out in hostelries over the centuries, places where people gather to celebrate or commiserate on the vicissitudes of life, or whether it is to do with the presence of other, equally potent, spirits, is debatable. However, the ex-landlord of the Old Gantondale Inn on the B1249 between Staxton and Foxholes is certain that malevolent spirits not only exist but were the cause of his bad luck.

The Old Gantondale already had a 'history' before Tony Nacey took it over. A 'grey lady' ghost had been seen, there was the sound of a phantom coach and horses, and rumours of a murder were prevalent in the area, although nothing was ever proved and no body found.

Eventually, in 1985, like so many haunted buildings, it was half-destroyed by a mysterious fire. While fighting the blaze firemen were disturbed by glimpses of a ghostly figure in the flames.

After the blaze the inn stood empty for a while and then Mr Nacey moved in and began renovation work. Whether or not he knew of the building's haunted history is unknown, but the force soon made its presence felt. The case is dealt with fully in Roy Palmer's *Britain's Living Folklore*, where Mr Nacey gives a long account of the haunting, describing how the evil atmosphere seemed to permeate the very fabric of the building. Although Mr Nacey had worked in many lonely and atmospheric buildings before, the inn at Gantondale held a peculiar terror for him. 'It was as though the building was crying,' he said, 'I used to dread coming in to work – the sight of it turned my stomach at one time.'

Then, just as quickly as it had begun, the haunting stopped, following the discovery of bones hidden in the wall. The Old Gantondale Inn is now open for business, its customers totally unaware of the malevolence the pub once played host to.

Mystery Animals in Yorkshire

The barguest or 'ghost dog' may be the most common alien animal encountered in Yorkshire, but there are other kinds of phantom creatures seen roaming the county. These seem to be displaced or mythical beasts which choose to manifest themselves in one geographical area for a short period of time before vanishing to become the stuff of legend.

No one knows exactly what flew over York in the early years of this millenium, but it was noted by Abbot Ralph that, 'Enormous footprints were supposedly left behind by the huge flying black horse that thundered across York during a lightning storm in 1065.' York being an old Viking city, it may well have been the Norse god Odin, leader of the spectral Wild Hunt, who was said to love riding the stormy skies on his eight-legged wind-horse, Sleipnir.

Old maps traditionally marked unknown areas with the phrase 'Here be dragons', using the image as a metaphor for the unexplored voids. Yorkshire has its dragon legends too, dating from the days when the countryside still held unknown terrors and the fight between good and evil was openly engaged. The Nunnington Worm legend is a classic example of a story full of hidden meanings and symbols, relevant to any interpretation of Yorkshire's dragon tales.

The tale is set at Midsummer's Eve in the age when the people of Nunnington in Ryedale had become Christianised but still held on to their pagan origins. All the villagers were there playing summer sports and watching the solstice bale-fire, and the queen of the festival was just about to be paraded around the streets, when a fierce hissing was heard coming from the surrounding forest.

A creature, half-serpent, half-dragon, followed the sound and slithered toward the village, its breath causing, in one old account of the legend, the air 'to become charged with a pestiferous influence'. In the ensuing chaos the festival queen was snatched by the worm, which henceforth acquired a taste for young females, and over the next few months took many more. Any men who tried to attack the dragon in its lair were overcome by its sulphurous breath.

Eventually a hero came forward. Sir Peter Loschy was said to be a pure Celt of direct descent from one of the knights of King Arthur, who had just returned from a three-year period of high adventure in the service of King Arthur. Loschy was told of the monstrous worm even before he arrived at Nunnington, and he realised that special equipment would be necessary to deal with this manifestation of evil.

To this end he travelled to Sheffield where he had a bespoke suit of armour fashioned with a coating of razors strong enough to repel any enemy, natural or otherwise. On his return to Ryedale he collected his magical sword, forged from Damascus steel, and set off to confront the dragon, his war-dog loping behind, eager for some dragon-slaying.

The worm had made its lair in a hill at East Newton which now bears the name Loschy Hill in memory of the duel. Combat was joined and raged all day, Loschy's magical sword hacking at the skin of the worm, severing scales and cutting coils. But this was to no avail, as each time a cut was made the monster rolled over on the ground whereupon the gashes instantly and magically healed. Nor could the dragon penetrate the razor guard of Loschy's suit of armour, and the battle between the Christian and the pagan forces continued unabated, neither side gaining an advantage.

After a while Loschy realised what was needed to complete the task and began to cut the worm into small pieces, as he did so commanding his dog to carry each piece to a separate location to prevent them rejoining the main body. Bit by bit the serpent was dismembered in this way, with the head eventually being taken to the site of Nunnington church.

Eventually the worm gave up the struggle, and the knight stood triumphant over its remains. In celebration of the victory, Loschy bent down to thank his dog but as he did so the dog jumped up and licked his face in affection, with disastrous results. As the dog had carried the head away, it had swallowed a quantity of the worm-venom, which was transferred to his master's face. The poison rapidly took effect and within minutes they were both dead.

The villagers mourned for days over the loss of their hero and eventually a commemorative stone was erected in Nunnington church, showing a knight with a dog at his feet. The tomb visible now is actually thought to be that of Sir Walter de Teyes, but legend claims it is Peter Loschy's.

Other dragon legends exist at Handale near Loftus, Sexhow, Kellington, and elsewhere in Yorkshire, and whatever their origin it is obvious that all dragon tales come from the same basic legend. In each case we have the same basic events: an evil dragon, a dragon's lair, breath which lays waste the fertility of the land, a knight who slays the dragon – often at the expense of sacrificing his own life – and the restoration of good and fertility to the people and their lands. These legends bear further investigation. Dragons may have vanished from the countryside, and if reports of sea-monsters from the east coast are to be believed, have gone back to the watery deeps.

Coastguard Wilkinson Herbert was a seasoned observer of the sea and hardly the type of man given to wild imaginings, so it came as a surprise to his friends and colleagues when he reported seeing a sea-serpent on Filey Brigg on 28 February 1934. Herbert was walking the shoreline when he was startled by a series of low growls coming from the beach in front of him. He shone his torch into the darkness and was confronted by a 'huge neck, six yards ahead of me, rearing up eight feet high'.

The monster seemed as shocked at this intrusion as Wilkinson Herbert was, but during the moments when they stared in disbelief at each other he observed that the body of the monster was about 9 metres long, black in colour and possessing four short legs, each with a huge flipper at the end. During this eerie torchlight examination, terror slowly crept over the coastguard and he wrote:

I thought 'this is no place for me' and from a distance I threw stones at the creature. It moved away growling fiercely . . . It moved quickly, rolling from side to side, and went into the sea. From the cliff top I looked down and saw two eyes like torchlights shining out to sea 300 yards away. It was a most gruesome and thrilling experience. I have seen big animals abroad, but nothing like this.

Further down the coast another sea creature was spotted at Easington, near Spurn Head. While strolling on the beach Joan Borgeest was startled to see a huge green creature rise from the waves, water dripping from its large flat head.

Mrs Borgeest reported that the sea-going leviathan had 'a flat head, protruding eyes and a long flat mouth which opened and shut as it breathed; it was a great length and moved along with a humped glide'. The monster slipped back beneath the waves as she shouted, trying to alert others on the beach. These are not the only sea-serpent sightings from the Yorkshire coast. A whole family saw the fast-moving head and humped body of a serpent off the coast at Hilston, swimming against the prevailing wind.

Flixton, on the A1039 road near Filey, was once haunted by a werewolf which would descend on unwary travellers as they passed through the region. In the manner of so many creatures from the otherworld this werewolf had glowing teeth and bright red eyes, and an appalling sulphurous stench hung about it.

A later Flixton legend tells of a travellers' hostel built there for shelter against the packs of wolves which roamed the area. But these were no ordinary wolves – this pack was supernaturally con-trolled by a magician who, in disguise, would mix with the local merchants and travellers, learn of their plans and then order his wolf pack to destroy them carrying the spoils back to him. Two legends may have become intertwined through the years, arising from travellers' fears of wolves and magicians and the image of the werewolf.

Perhaps it was this tale of wolves – real, imaginary or supernat-ural – which gave rise to the stories of out-of-place cats which have spread in Yorkshire since the Middle Ages, for example, the Barnburgh Cat. The legend centres on St Peter's Church at

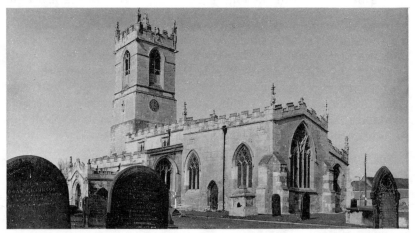

Barnburgh church, where a legendary 'wood cat' was killed in the porch in 1475

Barnburgh in South Yorkshire, where it is said Percival Cresacre died horribly at the claws of a 'wood cat' in 1475.

Cresacre was ambushed by the giant feline while out riding in the woods. The beast jumped up behind him and unseated him from the saddle. A terrible fight ensued with the cat locking itself onto the knight's back, causing him terrible injuries. He fought with the cat as he struggled all the way back to the church, losing blood and vital strength as he went. In a final act of will before death overtook him, he crushed the cat to death in the church porch. He was found next morning, frozen to the creature, by the church acolyte.

The heroic battle with this 'wood cat' went down in Cresacre family history and is embodied in their coat of arms, still to be seen on the tower of Barnburgh church. There are other relics there too, in the form of a carving of the event and stains on the church porch door, which are said to be those of blood resulting from the terrible struggle. No one has yet accounted for exactly what type of animal killed Cresacre. Wild cats were common at that time but it seems unlikely that one would grow large enough to attack and kill a fully-grown man, and this uncertainty, together with the knight's valour, has led to the growth of the legend.

Mystery 'big cats' have now taken over from wood cats. Since the 1930s there have been over 10,000 separate sightings and the number continues to rise each year. Yorkshire has been host to several of these transient escapees from some supernatural zoo.

In the autumn of 1981 Whitby was visited by a phantom feline which became known as the Whitby Lynx. A woman was woken in the early hours by unearthly screams and the sound of what later turned out to be her front-gate being torn to shreds. Upon inspection the following morning she discovered fang marks in the remains of the gate, but police were unable to tell her what sort of animal had the strength to do it, other than a big cat of some description.

The following evening a man walking his dog in the same area was confronted by a strange cat, much bigger than an ordinary species, with very long legs and pointed ears. It bared large, dog-like fangs at him and then slunk off into the night. The RSPCA was of the opinion the creature was a lynx and advised people not to corner it. Local police took a more practical view, a spokesman advising farmers to 'get out the twelve-bore and shoot it'.

The largest number of mystery cat sightings in Yorkshire were of the Harrogate Panther in 1985, when the mystery feline took up residence on retired farmer Richard Clifford's smallholding, just off the A59 Harrogate to Knaresborough road. Throughout October, Mr Clifford saw the animal clearly at least half a dozen times during the day, describing the cat as being the size of a small Alsatian dog, with a long tail and a low-slung belly. He was convinced that the creature had made a nest in the branches of an oak tree, and indeed an animal's den was later found there.

Over twenty other people also saw the Harrogate Panther. Many were regular walkers in the area, used to the local dogs and cats and so, they reasoned, unlikely to be confused. They all knew exactly what they had seen and it was a panther. Several witnesses independently verified Richard Clifford's account, even mentioning that they had seen the animal in the same tree. But there were many puzzling aspects to this case. If it had been any kind of flesh and blood animal, whether panther, wild cat or even domestic dog, there should have been evidence of its eating habits during its month long stay in the vicinity, for example droppings or tracks in the mud. Yet none were found, and the creature seen by so many people seemed to have no basis in physical reality.

Despite the sceptics' claims that this was just another incident of misperception, the police used tracker dogs, marksmen and even a police helicopter in the hunt for the elusive cat. They should have known better, for as soon as they stepped up their search, sightings dropped off rapidly and the panther retreated to its own dimension, leaving mystery and puzzlement in its wake.

Witches were once renowned for their ability to 'shape-shift' into the form of an animal, often a hare or a cat, and in 1984 a modern witch decided to demonstrate this ancient ability near the Pennine village of Heptonstall.

The witch, Barbara Brandolini from Manchester, had been attempting to purchase the derelict Baptist chapel at Slack for use as a pagan temple – a change of usage which horrified locals and church officials alike, and an argument raged with each side claiming their rights for religious freedom and tolerance. During this time a phantom panther had been sighted on the moorland borders between Yorkshire and Lancashire, resulting in the usual fruitless police searches and wild speculation. Several dead sheep had been discovered, eviscerated in a manner only found in the hunting habits of certain big cats, and farmers were out with their guns.

In a strange twist of the story Ms Brandolini claimed *she* was actually shape-shifting into the panther, and if the chapel were not sold to her she would appear in Heptonstall in panther form to make her powers felt.

It is not recorded whether or not she did materialise cat-like in the village, but the chapel was subsequently sold to another buyer and as usual the sightings of the big cat on the county border ceased shortly afterwards. Some may consider Ms Brandolini lucky, a beneficiary of our enlightened times. Anyone claiming the ability to change into an animal even a hundred years ago would have been imprisoned as a witch, and earlier still tortured and possibly executed.

It would appear that the phantom big cat has largely taken over from the earlier phantom, the black dog, in British folklore. Many aspects of the two creatures' appearance and behaviour are the same, and folklorists suspect one could be an updated story of the other. But does a folk tale kill sheep, or rip doors apart?

Big cats are one thing but both folklorists and sceptics found it difficult to know what could account for sightings of a native Australian animal in the suburbs of Bradford. In May 1982 a driver travelling into Bradford on the Shipley road had what can only be described as a 'close encounter of the furred kind'. As he approached Shipley a large animal ran, or rather hopped, in front of his car, causing him to slam the brakes on hard and screech to a halt. But it was too late, the animal hit the bumper and bounced off, revealing itself to be a large kangaroo which bounded off into Northcliffe Woods apparently unconcerned. Unable to believe his eyes the motorist carefully examined the front of his car and found tufts of hair and spots of blood in the radiator grill. These were sent for analysis but no further news of the missing marsupial was ever heard.

Perhaps Bradford has a secret colony of phantom marsupials living in its woods, because an almost identical incident took place seven years later, in 1989. A woman motorist driving down Hollins Hill at Guiseley was astounded when a 1.5-metre kangaroo suddenly came crashing down on her car, damaging the bonnet. Despite the bizarre nature of the accident and the obvious problems with any insurance claim, she called in the police, who took the incident very seriously. Police Sgt Dave Stockdale commented,

'The kangaroo just leaped over the wall and the woman motorist was unable to avoid it.'

Investigators of the paranormal often call an area which is prone to sightings of mystery craft or animals a 'window area', and with the spate of pterodactyl sightings which began in 1982 surely Bradford deserves such a title.

The first person to witness the creature saw it emerging from the Devil's Punchbowl, a small wooded area at the foot of Shipley Glen, one afternoon in September 1982. The first of hundreds of eye-witness accounts claimed:

It appeared to be flying in quite a haphazard manner, keeping fairly low. The silhouette was quite eerie. Its wings seemed to represent the shape of a bat or, more realistically, a pterodactyl!

Other reports spoke of the mystery bird as being grey with a pointed beak and short legs, and speculation was rife as to what it was. Sightings of the big bird flooded in to local newspapers, the *Bradford Telegraph and Argus* headline claiming 'Definitely no Heron', in answer to the sceptics who, having never witnessed the bird, had simply decided that it must be a heron. Others were equally convinced that it was either a bat, a hoaxer with a kite, or a genuine pterodactyl trapped in a time-warp. No evidence for any of these explanations was forthcoming and the bird continued to plague the outskirts of Bradford, unaware of the fuss it was causing down below.

Sightings increased. A Pudsey man, out walking his dog late one night, had a shock when he heard a banshee-like scream followed by a dull groaning sound. Looking round to identify the source of the noise he could see nothing. But then, as it was reported in the *Telegraph and Argus*:

The sounds were repeated, from roof-top level, and the man looked up to see a large bird towering above the chimney-pots on a neighbour's house. It was making the screaming call with its beak open, the grunt with its beak closed. As he watched, it launched itself from the roof, its weight causing it to drop below roof-level, before its slow wingbeat carried it off into the darkness.

Over the next few years there were intermittent sightings of the bird from areas between Bradford and Leeds. All the witnesses, without exception, were impressed with its size. In one of the final sightings, journalist Malcolm Hodds observed to colleague Mike Priestly that the bird was '. . . black and although hard to estimate size, I would say the wingspan was around five feet; there were feathers that looked like fingers on the end of the wings.' He seems to be describing a condor here, but condors simply don't exist, nor could they survive, in West Yorkshire. After Hodds' sighting the mystery bird just faded away. Perhaps a time-window opened and it returned to the prehistoric period from which it had come, but it vanished from sight if not memory, and the mystery has never been satisfactorily resolved.

It seems that whatever they are and wherever they come from, mystery animals move with the times. Whereas people once saw dragons and giant worms they now see sea-serpents, and where they once saw giant wild cats they now see lions and panthers, and so on. As our knowledge of the world and its mysteries expands we know that dragons can't exist and we replace them with more up-to-date terrors. Witnesses are numerous, evidence scarce and, especially in the case of people who reported a pterodactyl in twentieth-century Bradford, credulity is stretched to its limits. But these mystery animals exist for the people who see them, direct experience of an impossible nature which cannot be ignored.

Readers may think they have more chance of seeing the ghost of a human than a creature from the outer edges of reality, but this is exactly what all the witnesses in this chapter once thought. As writer John Keel says in his book *Strange Creatures from Time and Space*:

Belief or disbelief will come to you from another direction. Next week, next month, or next year you may be driving along a deserted country road late at night and as you round a bend you will suddenly see . . .

East Coast

Yorkshire's coastline is notable for its fine tourist resorts, but not so long ago it was famous for other activities. Smuggling was a major source of employment, carried on in parallel with the fishing activities for which towns such as Scarborough and Bridlington were noted. From fishing villages such as Whitby, ships sailed to the Arctic to hunt whale. Against this hardy seafaring background one would think that belief in ghosts and superstitions would have been eradicated by the harshness of life, but the reverse is possibly true, the coastal area of Yorkshire having a more varied selection of oddities than any of the other regions.

Boulby Cliffs near Staithes are over 182 metres and among the highest in the country. A ghost has been seen there walking precariously on the edge of the cliffs. It is the earthbound spirit of a girl killed during a landslip sometime in the nineteenth century. If she is seen it is thought unwise to approach her, as she walks not on the cliff top itself but a few metres out, on the level of the original cliff, and anyone trying to reach her will plunge to their death.

Hinderwell on the A174 is built around St Hilda's Church whose fifteenth-century chalice is one of the oldest in the country. David Naitby recorded that a witch once dwelt at Hinderwell who was famous for casting evil spells. A man named Slamper went to visit her for this reason and passing through the churchyard at nearby Roxby was:

> . . . set upon and hunted by a crowd of wraiths, who did hunt him over bog and dyke for about a mile, and then catching up with him did fairly judge him with many hard stripes from broom switches, the marks of which he bare on his skin to his death for all to admire and wonder at, and learn past all doubt the like be possible. This did happen in the year 1708.

Physical evidence of the supernatural realms was once common and people accepted that wraiths (spectres) existed with little or no comment.

One of the north's ubiquitous supernatural creatures, a hob, lived for a long time at Runswick Bay where he inhabited a small cave known as Hob Hole. The small hairy creature was paid due respect by people in the area and in return he granted cures, particularly to children suffering from whooping-cough, but only if the correct ritual was carried out. The patient would be taken to the cave and the following verse repeated by the parents: 'Hob-hole Hob! My bairn's gotten t'kink cough, Tak't off! Tak't off!' The supplicants rarely saw the hob but firmly believed in his existence, and the tradition continued well into this century.

Folklore, fact and fiction merge inextricably at the small sea hamlet of Kettleness, where the real experiences of an exorcist and the fictional memory of Dracula blend into a haunting which lasted over fifty years.

In the book *The Devil Hunter*, Donald Omand recalls that as a child a visit to Kettleness filled him with a nameless terror. The description he gives of the place could itself have come from a horror novel: 'Tiny child as I was, I recoiled from that place as if it had been Hell itself. It was a God-forsaken isthmus, peopled it seemed to me by a host of invisible demons.'

When he was older, Donald was excited to read in Bram Stoker's gothic horror novel *Dracula* the account of how the vampire came to be in England, as the result of a shipwreck off the Yorkshire coast at, of all places, Kettleness. Why here though? Curiously, the creature came ashore not as a vampire but in the form of a huge black dog.

Later, while he was working as a journalist on the *Northern Echo*, the Kettleness connection came back to haunt Omand when he was sent to do a story on a fisherman who had seen a ghostly black dog. The fisherman, a no-nonsense type, told his story simply. He had no reason to tell lies he said, but he had very definitely seen 'a great phantom dog' appear on Kettleness Point on many occasions.

But the story does not stop here. It seems that some people are plagued by a particular ghost all their life, and Donald Omand was bedevilled by Kettleness and its unearthly black dog. His next encounter with the haunted promontory took place during the 1950s, when he was a practicising exorcist and now a member of the clergy. He received a letter from a schoolmaster recounting how he and two friends had visited Kettleness where they had all seen a large black dog materialise from nowhere, suffusing the spot with an evil atmosphere. The schoolmaster's conclusion was that the apparition was a direct manifestation of evil which needed exorcism before the location would be psychically safe again.

Omand accepted the challenge and went straight to Kettleness accompanied by the schoolmaster and a bottle of holy water. Upon arrival he once again noted the same sense of evil he had experienced as a child, and as they stood surveying the elemental seascape before them, Omand quipped, 'All we need now is for Dracula to come bounding ashore in the form of a great black dog.' As he uttered these words the schoolmaster stiffened with terror. A large black dog materialised from the sea-air and began bounding toward them. In Omand's words, 'What we saw looked like a huge black hound, but bigger than any of the canine species known to man.'

His companion fled back to the comparative safety of the car, but despite being terrified the Revd Omand composed himself to complete the job he had travelled there to perform. He exorcised the advancing devil-hound with the words: 'Be gone in the name of the Lord Jesus Christ. Be gone to the place appointed for you, there to remain forever. Be gone in the name of Christ.'

The phantom hound vanished on contact with the consecrated water and the exorcist went on to purify the area where the creature had been seen, commenting in his account of the episode: 'the menace of Kettleness was ended. The corruption had departed.'

Kettleness today is still an atmospheric location, one which in its wildness and proximity to the power of the sea evokes in even the most rational person a sense that the boundaries between worlds may be thin. Perhaps Bram Stoker had sensed this atmosphere too and created a 'thought-form' at the spot, one that could be seen by those with the equivalent of second sight.

Whitby is dominated by the ancient abbey which stands on the south side of the harbour, reached by climbing the 199 steps from Church Street. The steps are known locally as Jacob's Ladder, and it is claimed to be impossible to count them correctly.

On the beach below the abbey, fossil ammonites can be found, tiny coiled serpent-like creatures from the Jurassic period. One legend which sprang up to account for them, in the days before geology was a science, suggested that they came to be there because on St Hilda's arrival at Whitby Abbey she found the entire area infested with poisonous snakes, which she drove off the edge

Whitby Abbey, haunted by St Hilda and a spectral monk's singing

of the cliff. As they fell she knocked their heads off and they curled themselves into small balls, forming the familiar circular fossil ammonites which have now been incorporated in the town's coat of arms. The area on which the abbey stands is named Haggerlythe; hag, hagger or hag worm are old country names for an adder.

St Hilda's ghost has frequently been seen in the abbey grounds, and one theory claims that if one stands on the west side of the churchyard she can be seen standing in one of the northern windows of the abbey, clad in a shroud. Ghostly singing can sometimes be heard wafting through the abbey. Caedmon, a former monk, was visited in the abbey stables by an angel who gave him the gifts of singing and the composition of music. She also instructed him that his first song should be of the Creation.

Although the abbot was sceptical about this apparent miracle, he told the monk the Creation story in full and Caedmon wrote a song on the spot, singing it in an angelic voice in front of his fellow monks. The most auspicious time for hearing this spectral song is at daybreak on Christmas Day, when it may be heard accompanied by a choir of angels.

Whitby has several minor ghosts about which little is known. For instance Prospect Hill has the ghost of a headless man. Unusually for headless ghosts, this one has his head tucked firmly beneath his arm. A mischievous spirit in the form of a hob has been known to make life difficult for motorists on the outskirts of Whitby, causing skids and altering road signs, and just inland between Ruswarp and Sleights, the ghost of a village idiot can be found. Known as Goosey as the result of his worldly habit of eating an entire goose in one meal, he wanders the B1410 road, eternally looking for any stray geese.

Anyone wanting to make a wish should visit the 'wishing chair' at the end of Love Lane in Whitby. This chair, in reality an old cross base, may grant any wish to the sitter. It can be found occupying the somewhat mundane position of guarding a telephone box outside a launderette, and is largely ignored by the local children, who now wish for things beyond even the powers of a wishing chair.

The ever-present threat of the sea combined with the age-old fear of witchcraft led many fishermen to carry charms to ward off evil influences. The famous black Whitby jet was believed to have magical properties and was worn as protection, fashioned into a variety of shapes according to the beliefs of the wearer. It could also be burnt as a type of incense to stave off evil. Other evil-averting charms used by east coast fisherfolk included wearing a certain bone found in a sheep's head. The bone is called the 'Hammer of Thor' due to its similarity to a hammer, and the name harks back to the days of the Norse settlers in the area and their belief in the god Thor.

Two old halls at Whitby are said to be haunted. Aisalby Hall has two classic hauntings in the shape of a 'white lady' who wanders forever through the rooms and passages dressed in a long dress, and a phantom coach and horses which rushes up to the door and immediately disappears. No explanation or origin for these two ghosts has ever come to light, although the ghostly coach may well be related to Whitby's other phantom coach, which careers wildly along the coast road before plunging out of control over the cliffs.

Poltergeist phenomena have been reported from Bagdale Old Hall on Baxtergate, where objects were moved about by supernatural agency and odd noises were heard. Ghost-hunter Antony Hippisley Cox reports that the hall, now a hotel, was left empty for many years, made uninhabitable by its unseen but noisy ghostly residents.

At Ascentiontide an intriguing custom is still carried out on the foreshore at Whitby. In what to an ignorant onlooker must seem a complete waste of time, a hedge is painstakingly constructed on the beach at Boyes Staith. This is known as the Planting of the Penny Hedge, or the Horngarth. The hedge must be strong enough to withstand the impact of three tides, and is traditionally made from osiers cut at sunrise on Ascension Eve from a local woodland. This curious ceremony dates back to 1159, when a hermit was beaten to death by three drunken hunters while at his devotions. To avoid being executed for the crime the men who committed the murder were given the penance of building the hedge each year, their descendants continuing the practice. The name Penny Hedge is derived from 'penance hedge'.

Although folklorist J. Fairfax-Blakeborough said that nowadays no one has 'sufficient faith, poetry, romance – call it what you will – to see the tiny, graceful sprites', fairies were once common in the coastal villages, taking their place alongside the hobs, barguests and brownies.

Thomas Rogers' diary for 7 May 1650 recounts the experiences of Ralph Blackburn and friends near Whitby, where they all 'espied many fairies disporting themselves right merrily. They watched them for some time, until one, dancing a little space from the ring, discovered them, when, giving a signal, they all departed on the instant.' Nowadays anyone claiming to have seen fairies would be considered slightly odd. In those times this sighting was regarded

Bagdale Old Hall, now a hotel, was left unoccupied for many years because of poltergeist activity

with joy and respect, Rogers' diary going on to say that: 'This pleaseth the townsfolk greatly.'

In fields between Whitby and Hawkser were two stone monoliths known as Robin Hood's Arrows. Charlton's *History of Whitby* notes that they were fired there by the famous outlaw from the roof of Whitby Abbey. Robin had been invited there along with Little John to have dinner with the monks and loosed the arrows to demonstrate his prowess with the bow. In reality these stones are Bronze Age standing stones – far too old for the legends of Robin Hood which sprang up in the Middle Ages – and the distance is over one mile, out of the range of even the best of today's archers. The tradition is further entrenched with the fields being named Robin Hood's Field and John's Field respectively. The connection between Robin, ancient monuments and Christian buildings hints yet again at the figure being a legendary survival of a pagan god whose feats were attached to earlier religious monuments.

Robin Hood's Bay, six miles to the south of Whitby, is said to have gained its name from the time when the outlaw stayed there during a visit to the east coast. Leland's *Itinerary* refers to the cluster of houses hanging from the hillsides as 'a fischer tounlet of 20 bootes caullid Robyn Huddes Bay, a dok or bosom of a mile in length'. Before moving on to Scarborough Robin spent time practising his archery skills at Robin Hood's Butts, prehistoric burial mounds on nearby Howdale Moor.

The outlaw's stay in Scarborough is described in the ballad, 'The Noble Fisherman' which opens with Robin making a decision:

The fishermen brave more money have
Than any merchants two or three;
Therefore I will to Scarborough go,
That I a fisherman brave may be.

According to the ballad, while in Scarborough Robin stayed with a widow woman under the assumed name of Simon Wise and soon found work on a fishing boat. The ballad goes on to poke fun at Robin and his land-locked ways, the ship's master telling him that he will never be any use on a boat. The crew soon change their minds, however, when they are attacked by a French warship. As the captain bemoans the imminent loss of his ship and possibly his life, Robin reveals his identity and creates havoc among the French crew with his longbow. The French are all killed, resulting in the

Scarborough fishermen capturing the boat and 12,000 pieces of gold which, the ballad tells us, Robin donates for the building of 'a dwelling for th'oppressed'.

If Robin Hood was a flesh and blood outlaw he would have no doubt visited the Three Mariners Tavern during his stay in the port. It was traditionally a smugglers' inn and the haunt, quite literally, of a headless woman. She is said to have been the wife of a drowned sailor, although the tales never make it clear quite how she lost her head. Any fisherman who saw the spectre would refuse to go out to sea on that day, as her appearance presaged disaster, and stories are told of foolhardy fisherfolk who flouted this superstition being lost at sea as a result. The Three Mariners is now a museum, packed with artefacts from times gone by in the fishing port, and the ghost's appearances are no longer dreaded.

Just as Whitby is dominated by its abbey so Scarborough is guarded by the castle, which occupies the high promontory dividing the north and south bays. There has been some form of building on this spot since at least the Bronze Age, and it is still possible to see

Scarborough Castle is built on an ancient site and has witnessed many unexplained phenomena

Filey Brigg – the Devil's handiwork?

evidence of pre-Christian habitation there in the form of the holy well. Named Our Lady's Well, it is described in the castle guide-book as having waters 'once held to be miraculous'.

One of the many episodes of violence to which the castle was witness was the treacherous beheading of Piers Gaveston, who was tricked into surrendering the castle in return for his supposed freedom. Earthbound, Gaveston's headless spectre parades what is left of the battlements when the castle is closed at night. Scarborough Castle would also have provided an ideal vantage point from which to look out for the ghostly black horse which has been reported in the skies above the town for almost a thousand years.

Filey is famous for its Brigg, the long reef which cuts out into the North Sea for almost a mile. It was reputedly made by the Devil. While engaged in one of his many supernatural building projects, he dropped his hammer and formed the reef while groping around in the water. Another version of its creation suggests it is the skeletal remains of a dragon.

Filey once had a reputation for lawlessness and distrust of religion. Occasionally, visiting members of the clergy would be pelted with rotted fish and vegetables, even as late as the nineteenth century. It is said that the town was finally converted by a Bridlington priest known as Praying Johnny, who achieved his aim by falling to his knees and praying to God not to let him be embarrassed, as he had already told his Bridlington flock that he would win the Filey disbelievers over. God granted him his wish and the people of Filey subsequently became devout Christians.

Cole, in his *History of Filey*, recounts a strange Easter custom once held there in which the young men stole the shoes from any females they could find on one day and on the following day the females stole the hats from any young men they met. All items were later ritually returned at a special celebratory supper.

Down the coast at Flamborough a ghost named Jenny Gallows only appears to children, who once used to be very careful not to disturb the spirit with their noisy games. If she was woken from her rest the ghost would chant this rhyme: 'Ah'll put on mi bonnet, An tee on mi shoe, An if thoo's not off, Ah be after thoo.' The name Jenny is a common one throughout the north of England in connection with ghosts and place guardians, and is probably the name of an old pagan nature spirit. Children in the Yorkshire Dales were often threatened with Jenny Greenteeth if they did not behave and Jenny Gallows seemed to fulfil a similar function on the coast.

The headland at Flamborough is bisected by an ancient earthwork named Danes Dyke, after the legend that it was built by the Danes on one of their many landings on the east coast. The clearly visible entrenchment is haunted by a 'white lady' type of apparition. Near the dyke the cliffs which encircle the north landing are riddled with caves once used by the smuggling fraternity, and one famous smuggler, Robin Lythe, was found washed up at sea in one of the caves there, according to legend.

Local people took him in and he became a notorious smuggler in the area. The cave where he was found is called Robin Lythe's Cave, and can be reached on foot at low tide on the south side of the landing. At night the north landing is a wild and lonely place with little to suggest that it is now a twentieth-century tourist

Danes Dyke is frequented by a 'white lady' apparition

location. The ghosts seem unaware of this too, and there have been reports of phantom ships coming aground at night, with the noise of illegal cargo being unloaded and the voices and footfalls of the spectral smugglers clearly heard on the shingle.

Pennel's Pool, off the coast of Yorkshire, is an area once assiduously avoided by fishermen. This part of the sea, now nearly a hundred metres offshore, was part of the mainland in the eighteenth century. On the cliffs there in 1770 a pirate by the name of Pennel was hung in a gibbet following his execution in London. His body, bound in iron, was visible for miles around and hung in the sea winds for years as a mute warning to would-be pirates and smugglers. As the sea encroached, both cliff and gibbet were overtaken but an area of turbulence at the spot remains and both memory and name ensure that wise seafarers avoid the place, for Pennel's ghost is said to be waiting beneath the surface to draw unwary sailors under.

St John of Bridlington was once famed for his miracles, and besides healing the lame and restoring sight to the blind, John rescued a party of Hartlepool sailors after they had been blown off-course during a storm. As they were about to be dashed to their deaths on the rocks at Flamborough Head, one of the crew saw

Bridlington Priory in the distance and offered a prayer to John for help and deliverance of their souls. The amazed sailors were saved from certain death by John walking through the towering waves to reach them, and pulling the boat by its prow to safety in the harbour at Bridlington.

Stories of the sea overshadow most others on the east coast and even today fishermen, when faced with its power and mystery, can be superstitious. When the crew of the Bridlington trawler *Pickering* didn't seem to be going to sea very often, the Department of Social Security conducted an investigation and uncovered a tale which could have been straight from the Middle Ages. Chillingly, it was from 1987.

When questioned as to this apparent lack of desire to work, the skipper said in defence of his crew that they could no longer stand being on board the boat as it was haunted. He cited lights flickering on and off, permanently freezing cabin temperatures, faulty steering and erratic radar as evidence of this unlikely claim.

Crewman Barry Mason had actually seen the apparition of a flat-cap-wearing figure on deck late at night. The previous skipper was also consulted, and recounted experiencing similar problems in an interview with *Fishing News* adding, 'My three months on the the *Pickering* were the worst in seventeen years at sea, I did not earn a penny because things were always going wrong and no one could understand or explain why.'

The DSS's investigation surprisingly concluded that these were good reasons for not going out to sea, but investigators were at a loss as to how to resolve the problem. In times past these fishermen would have known exactly what to do: visit the local witch or wise man to remove the ghost. Sadly, these mediators between the worlds are no longer available, but a DSS official arranged for an exorcist to deal with the problem. Bridlington vicar Tom Willis sailed with the *Pickering* and conducted an exorcism at sea during December 1987. The crew was impressed, skipper Gates saying: 'Next day we sensed a totally different atmosphere. It was warm and friendly and since then we have not had problems and had very successful fishing trips.'

Research into the vessel's past conducted by the Revd Willis revealed what may have been the cause of the haunting. The *Pickering* had once been registered in southern Ireland as the *Family Crest* and during this time a crewman had been lost at sea.

East Yorkshire

A hair salon may seem an unusual place for a haunting, but that is just what was reported from the White Rose Salon on Whitefriargate in Hull. Mysterious noises had been heard in the building for a number of years, reaching new levels during 1971 when customers and staff heard the sound of feet walking to and fro across an empty upstairs room. Eventually the owners became so perturbed that they called the police in, who rigged the room with trip wires and sealed the door. But this did little to deter the ghost, which persisted in its mysterious draggings and shufflings, and when the police finally opened the door again they found the trip wires untouched but the light mysteriously on.

'I had a funny thing happen four years ago,' Hull resident Mrs Exley wrote in a letter to researcher Ian Taylor, going on to recall how she had encountered a strange creature in a field near her home. 'It was utterly black, with pointed ears and a head like a lioness's. What impressed me most was that this animal was so flat, like two dimensional.' The dog stopped and looked at her, but was curiously ignored by Mrs Exley's own dog, which normally would never have let another animal near him.

Later that same day her mother saw the dog in their garden, and at 10.30 pm when her father was letting their dog back in from the garden, he commented, 'That queer dog's just walked up the garden path alongside our dog.' The black dog just faded away as their own dog entered the house. It was then that Mrs Exley realised why her dog had not challenged the intruder – he couldn't see or smell it. The ghost dog of the northern counties had made another appearance and Mrs Exley's final words on the matter were, 'Three weeks later my dad collapsed and died. I knew then with certainty that the black dog was some sort of weird being.'

Pocklington's claim to fame is a gruesome one, and one which we should not be proud of, for it was the site of the last 'legal' witch-burning in England. The parish register for 1631 records that 'Old Wife Green was burnt in the market square for acts of witchcraft'.

The nearby village of Warter once had an inn called 'The

Creeping Kate'. It is now a sub-post office, but a local tradition hints that the original pub had a tunnel to Cross Green. The cellars of the post office are haunted by a ghost which is felt rather than seen.

On the Everingham to Pocklington road there have been persistent sightings of a phantom cyclist. Shortly before the Second World War, Police Constable Moody chased a black-clad cyclist along this road to caution him for riding without lights. As he closed in on the figure, which he sensed to be female, she took a right turn and vanished. The constable was overcome with a sensation of icy cold and he knew instantly he had seen a ghost.

He researched the area's history and discovered that a woman cyclist had been run down on that road. Other sightings have been made and all have noted that the spectre vanishes at the same spot – the entrance to Everingham Hall. Strangely enough, a cook from the hall drowned herself near this spot and is said to haunt the same spot as the ghostly cyclist.

Spaldington Hall, once an Elizabethan mansion, has been replaced by a nineteenth-century farmhouse but the centuries-old haunting at the location continues. It began when a practical joker was kicked downstairs and killed in the hall during the reign of James I. His ghost seems to have mutated into a hob, a mischievous sprite which disrupted daily life at the hall for years. In a time-honoured tradition the legend says that the ghost or hob was laid with a willow stake and was banished to a well for three generations.

Three generations is hardly a long time for a timeless spirit, and the current farmhouse is still beset by poltergeist phenomena. Ian Taylor interviewed the occupants and was told that, 'Robin is back out of the well again.' Further credence is given to this story by the fact that a well does exist in the grounds of the farm. The idea of trapping a ghost in water, especially a well, is common throughout East Yorkshire. In *The Ancient Springs and Streams of the East Riding of Yorkshire*, written in 1923, the Revd Smith notes that, 'At Garton's Well, Robin (a hob) was imprisoned by the aid of charms for ninety-nine years and a day, ninety-nine nails being driven into the door of the mill to 'attest the fact'.'

Elizabeth Gutch in *Folklore of the North Riding* noted that in the churchyard of St Catherine's at Barmby Moor there was a 'rude rough stone six feet long and 22 to 15 inches wide . . . Tradition

The 'wart stone' at St Catherine's Church, Barmby Moor, has long been used for its curative powers

The ancient barrow of Willy Howe is said to be inhabited by fairies

says it was a certain cure for warts.' This was in 1901 but the stone still stands, and the water contained in small depressions on the side and top still has curative powers. Ian Taylor mentions that he was cured of two warts by this method, and the author tried this cure in January 1992 and was pleasantly surprised to find that a wart on his right index finger vanished within days. The old countryfolk certainly knew things we have forgotten.

Willy Howe, near the village of Wold Newton on the north side of the Wolds, is a Neolithic round barrow. At 7 metres high and 39 metres across it is one of the largest in Britain, and was once well-known as a haunt of fairies and so avoided.

During the reign of Richard I a local man chanced to ride past the haunted mound and as he did so he heard sweet, enchanting music issuing from it. Curious, he approached the hill, and through a door which opened in the side he could see into a fabulous banqueting hall where fairies drank and feasted. He tried to slip away unnoticed but it was too late. He was offered a drink, but just in time realised that drinking from a fairy vessel would be stupid, as this would bind him to the place and so he made as if to take the drink but instead snatched the goblet from the fairy's hand and fled.

The fairies set off in hot pursuit but he managed to escape with his trophy. People who examined the cup proclaimed it to be of 'fairy gold' and thus worthless, while others commented on its unusual shape and colour and also on the fact that it was fashioned from an unknown material. The goblet was held in such high regard that it was eventually presented to the King. Unfortunately, nothing has been heard of it since, but for those who doubt the story a visit to Willy Howe on a moonlit night is recommended.

Wold Newton's prophetic spring, the Gypsey Race, flows intermittently due to the nature of the geology and depending on the rainfall. In the past this erratic behaviour led people to believe that supernatural forces controlled the water's flow and that whenever it flowed copiously a disaster would follow.

The legend was first mentioned in the chronicle of William of Newborough, who wrote during the reign of Henry II:

. . . in East Yorkshire . . . famous springs of water arise. They do not flow perpetually, but intermittently. When the springs are dry it is a good sign, for when they flow it is undoubtedly a sign of coming famine.

Inhabitants of Burton Fleming, through which the Gypsey Race flows, once had a tradition that as soon as the waters began to flow the young folk of the village would run out to meet it, perhaps in an abortive attempt to stop its malign influence, and offerings to propitiate the water spirits may have been made at one time. On the subject of the legend and its prophecy it is recorded that the waters, once known colloquially as 'Woe Waters', were full immediately prior to the Great Plague of 1666, both World Wars and sundry other world disasters. But as Cooper writes in *Curiosities of East Yorkshire*, 'If Augustus could trace the defeat of his army to the fact that the sacred chickens refused to eat their food, a resident of North Burton may as reasonably attribute the death of his cow to the flow of the Gypsey Race.'

The Gypsey Race flows through Rudston, where the standing stone situated in the churchyard is the tallest in Great Britain and well worth a visit. It is 7.7 metres tall, 1.8 metres wide and 76 cm thick, and may have originally been even taller, as there appears to be a piece missing from the top. Tradition claims that there is as much again beneath the ground and the total weight could be up to 40 tons. Although the church is of Norman origin, the stone is dated as being up to 3,600 years old and presumably marks a site of great sanctity. The fact that the church was built so near adds to this speculation, and suggests the Christians recognised and made use of an already sacred location. One of the legends about the stone is that it was hurled there by the Devil in an attempt to destroy the church, but as usual his aim was poor and the missile fell short.

The year 1844 was famous throughout Yorkshire for its peculiar meteorological phenomena. In June of that year something conspired with the elements to give what Mayhew, in his *Annals of Yorkshire*, recorded thus:

At Selby, with the fall of rain, there was a shower of frogs. Several were caught in their descent by holding out hats for that purpose. They were about the size of a horse bean and remarkably lively after their aerial but wingless flight.

Flying frogs are not the only aerial phenomena to have attained legendary status in the region. Just to the south-west of Wold

The mysterious monolith in Rudston churchyard is the tallest standing stone in Great Britain

Newton stands an obelisk erected in 1797 to mark the spot where a 31-kg meteorite fell to earth.

Witches were as common in East Yorkshire as anywhere else, and just as feared. Evidence of this witch-hatred can be found in Welton Dale, where it is recorded that there is an old twisted thorn tree set apart from any other. It is easily recognisable because its branches are weighed down with stones. Deborah Tinkler was stoned to death at this spot for casting enchantments on her husband and the stones are those which missed her during the barbaric punishment.

Witches were also believed to have the power to stop horses and carts, and one Wolds clergyman clearly recalls an old woman telling him in dialect about one such instance and the remedy:

111

Wickenwood's t'stuff they mak' whipstocks on ti scare witches. Yance some lads were comin' wi' carts, an' ez seaan ez they comed nigh-hand a brif t'fosst draught was stopped, t'hosses couldn't storr, till yan o't'lads with a wicken-tree gad comes up; then away they went. T'witch couldn't stop 'em then.

At one time 'wicken-tree gads', or rowan tree sticks, were openly sold at fairs and market towns in the area for just such a purpose.

Hobs and goblins of all types once roamed east Yorkshire, offering help or sometimes hindrance to farmers and landowners. East Yorkshire hobs could be vindictive if scorned, as one Holderness farmer discovered to his cost. Nothing would placate the bad-tempered hob and so in desperation the farmer packed his belongings and made ready to leave the farm and the hob behind.

As the horse and cart moved off from the hob-infested farm, the farmer's neighbour saw them and called out, 'Is tha flitting?' but before his friend could reply a voice came from the back of the cart, 'Aye we're flitting!' The hob sat grinning on a milk churn and the farmer unloaded the cart, resigned to life with the vindictive hob. But later, by the aid of protective charms, the luckless farmer was able to lure the hob into a well, where he remained trapped, and the well is known to this day as Robin Round Cap Well.

In medieval times 1,300-year-old Beverley Minster was a place of sanctuary for fugitives. King Athelstan granted the privilege of sanctuary, saying, 'It shall be a sanctuary, with a Fridstool before the altar, as a place of refuge and safety for debtors and criminals.' The boundaries of protection extended a mile in each direction and were marked by a stone. The fridstool or frithstool is a large chair carved from stone which is still situated to the right of the altar. People obtaining sanctuary had thirty days to obtain a pardon, and during their stay were provided with food and sometimes accommodation by the clergy.

Beverley Minster is rumoured to have several secret tunnels, one of which is said to stretch to the site of Holderness Abbey of Meaux, while another ran to the Holy Well at Kilnwick. But perhaps the most important one provided a link with Watton Abbey, which is haunted by the ghost of a nun named Elfrida who was seduced by a monk and bore his child. Despite doing penance for her alleged sins, she was executed but was later forgiven by the Archbishop of York. This must have been small comfort to her

Beverley Minster, a sanctuary in medieval times, is said to have several secret tunnels

spirit, and in revenge she haunts the grassy mound which now marks the remains of the abbey. Headless ghosts are also said to haunt the abbey mounds, those of a woman and child murdered during a raid by parliamentarians following the battle of Marston Moor.

The hill on the side of Nafferton Slack once had an enormous stone which was believed to have fantastic powers. It was ostensibly there to prevent wagons running off the road, but it seems to have had a magical significance prior to this. At night the stone would light up and people often saw troops of fairies entering and leaving on foot or in horses and carriages. It was thought that the stone was an entrance to the underworld. Another more recent legend connected with a hill concerns the ghost coach of Garrowby Hill. Following a tragic accident there in August 1931 in which two people were killed, talk began to circulate of a phantom vehicle which appeared on the hill. All who saw the vehicle encountered it at or near the site of the accident and on the anniversary of the crash in August.

The headless ghost of a woman haunts a stretch of road between Leven and Riston. She petrifies unsuspecting travellers by jumping up behind horsemen and clapping their ears. The road at Frodingham is also haunted, by a headless man who once accompanied a rider home from the pub, sharing his saddle. One of the more interesting sightings of this road ghost comes from 1937, when a travelling salesman was returning overnight to his home at Harpham just as dawn broke.

As Robert Weir drove through Frodingham in the early morning light he noticed a horse and rider ahead of him, and slowed so as not to frighten the horse. But as he tried to overtake he realised that he did not seem to be gaining on the rider, who remained about 90 metres in front. He accelerated up to speeds of 40 mph but still the hooded rider kept his distance. By now a few miles had passed and Weir realised the rider was not as he seemed. In a final attempt to determine exactly what he was dealing with he sounded his horn. At this the rider reigned the horse in and slowly turned. Beneath the hood Weir could see a skeletal death's head peering out at him and in terror he ran his car off the road into the ditch. He was found unconscious at 10 o'clock that morning by the village policemen, to whom he told his story.

St John of Beverly was born in Harpham in the seventh century and he may have preached at the holy well there, known as the Drumming Well, situated in a field behind the church. The well is now somewhat overgrown and neglected, but even recently people have heard a strange noise emanating from it. The noise, a persistent drum beat, is the result of a drummer-boy named Tom being knocked head-first into the well. His mother, the village wise woman, claimed that whenever a villager was going to die the death would be foretold by her son drumming from the bottom of the well. This legend and the fact that it is stipulated he went in 'head-first' may be a folk memory of the time when human sacrifice and the offering of skulls and heads were carried out at holy wells.

Many parts of the country have houses or farms which possess an object whose removal will cause disaster to the house, animals, crops or occupants. These objects become guardians or protective spirits of the building. At Crowle, for instance, there is a large black stone in a farmyard which the farmer will not remove, despite the inconvenience it causes, for fear of supernatural retribution.

However, that is a simple story compared with the complex guardian legend of seventeenth-century Burton Agnes Hall. The hall is the family seat of the Boyntons and the story concerns Anne Boynton, who supervised the rebuilding of the hall, taking great pride and pleasure in watching the work as it progressed. Unfortunately, she was never to see it completed. Returning from a visit to the St Quentin family at nearby Harpham, Anne was stopped by two beggars who savagely attacked her when she would not part with a ring she was wearing.

Anne was brought back to Burton Agnes Hall and over the next few days drifted in and out of a coma. She must have realised death was near as her only words in her few lucid moments concerned the hall she loved. She told her family that she could not rest in the grave unless some part of her remained at the hall, and made them promise that when she died her head would be severed and kept at the hall. In order to pacify her the family agreed and Anne died peacefully, but her body was buried in one piece.

A legendary skull, bricked up in a secret location in Burton Agnes Hall, acts as its guardian spirit

Barely a week after the funeral, ghostly noises began to permeate the house, followed by screams and hand-clapping. This disturbance continued week after week on the anniversary of Anne's death and became so frightening that the servants could stand it no more and left the hall. Anne's sisters conferred with the vicar and, remembering their sister's final wish, they decided to open the coffin.

Despite several weeks having passed since the burial, Anne's body was in perfect condition, but what horrified them was the fact that the head was now neatly but mysteriously severed from the body in accordance with Anne's wishes, and was almost fleshless. The sisters were certain this was because they had not obeyed Anne's dying wish and lost no time in taking the skull back to the hall, where it was placed on a table and the disturbances stopped.

Over the years many attempts were made to rid the hall of the grisly relic, but each time the ghostly noises came back and the skull was returned to its rightful place in the hall. On one occasion a maid-servant hurled the skull out of a window on to a passing load of manure, but the horses stopped and refused to move until the skull was removed and taken back inside. Other attempts to give it away or bury it in consecrated ground all failed, and eventually, to avoid any further possibility of 'Awd Nance', as she was known, returning, the skull was bricked up in a secret location at the hall to become its guardian forever.

South Yorkshire

When the church of St Luke and All Saints at Darrington was damaged by storms in 1895, an examination of the foundations was made which uncovered grisly evidence of a foundation sacrifice beneath the west side of the tower. According to the *Yorkshire Herald* of 31 May 1895:

> The grave must have been prepared and the wall placed with deliberate intention upon the head of the person buried, and this was done with such care that all remained as placed for at least 600 years.

This discovery is typical of the foundation offerings found in churches throughout the country. Most offerings were of animals and it is rare to find a human body offered in this way. In this case the sacrifice may have already been dead, but it is a direct reminder of the days when a life was willingly given up to bestow luck on a new building.

A ghost known as Lindholme Willy was seen on numerous occasions on the former airfield at Lindholme Moss, which closed in the 1970s. The apparition always appeared in full flying gear, as though it had just stepped from a plane, and it was believed that Willy was a Polish airman who died when a badly damaged Lancaster bomber crashed and exploded in nearby Hatfield Waste.

Older ghosts haunt the area too, and long before the airfield was built, Lindholme was home to William de Lindholme, a hermit whose grave was found in 1727 near Lindholme Hall. His ghost once stalked the marshes but was superseded by the phantom airman, and it would be an interesting line of research to ascertain how many sites with modern ghosts have previously been haunted by more ancient spectres. The site of the airfield is now a prison, and it can only be a matter of time before inmates begin to report ghostly happenings there.

During the early years of this century the parish church at Doncaster was the scene for a number of hauntings which raise the question 'which is haunted – witness or location?' The hauntings began when the Revd Morgan took over the incumbency. One of the first experiences concerned a ghostly gurgling noise which occurred one night when he was alone in the vicarage, waking him instantly. The following morning he asked his housekeeper what the noise could have been, and was shocked when she replied, 'I couldn't stay in the house since the day the poor man killed himself in your bedroom.' The suicide had hanged himself when he was refused marriage by the daughter of a previous vicar at the church.

One particular grave in the churchyard seemed to be the focus of paranormal activity, and on many occasions the vicar discovered a skull at the side of the tombstone. Each time he pushed it back beneath the earth again, thinking it had been unearthed by rats or other scavengers, but it would always reappear at the side of the stone.

The skull demonstrated its powers fully during the latter years of the First World War. The clergyman was woken suddenly one morning by someone banging on the door of the vicarage, who turned out to be a soldier demanding to know what lay on the other side of the garden wall. While passing through the graveyard he had seen a ghostly figure rise from beneath a gravestone, run through the graves and jump over the wall. Knowingly the vicar showed the soldier what was behind the wall: a 5.4-metre drop into a schoolyard. When the soldier pointed out the tomb from which the figure had risen, the vicar was not surprised to find it was the grave with the wandering skull.

The vicarage was later demolished, it is said, because no one would live there due to the ghosts, but it is worth noting that the Revd Morgan had had many ghostly experiences prior to living in Doncaster, his earliest being when he was nine. In cases like this it is hard to determine whether the haunting is of the place or the person.

Perhaps Doncaster's strangest paranormal encounter took place in the late 1970s at the height of punk rock. At that time the popular group X-Ray Specs, fronted by singer Poly Styrene, were in the town. As they finished a performance at the Outlook Club Ms Styrene saw a UFO. She later said of the experience, 'I just had to go on searching for more knowledge. Inevitably it's going to lead to religion in the end.' The experience had a profound effect on the singer, triggering off a religious quest which ended when she became a follower of the Hari Krishna sect.

St Michael's Church at Rossington dates from Norman times and still retains many features from that period. Somewhere in the churchyard there is the unmarked grave of James Boswell who died in 1702. Boswell was a gypsy king and latter-day Robin Hood who went to live in Sherwood Forest, where he worked to improve the life of gypsies and travelling folk, becoming so popular that he was revered almost as a god. When he was laid to rest gypsies and country-folk would travel from miles around to chip off a piece of his gravestone as a good luck charm, with the result that the gravestone eventually vanished altogether.

Drinkers in the Eagle and Child at Auckley might question the strange juxtaposition in the pub's name. Perhaps they would be more curious if it was widely known that the pub was originally called the Bird and the Bastard. This even more unlikely combination has its origins in a village legend from the fourteenth century, when the surrounding land was owned by Sir Thomas Latham. In his desperate search for a son and heir he seduced a serving girl who gave birth to a boy. However, due to his sense of morality he did not want this revealed and instead had the child 'abandoned' at the foot of a tree in which nested a bird of prey he was studying. The child was then 'found' by him and so could legitimately be adopted, giving rise to the peculiar original name of the inn.

Hickleton village stands on the route of the old Streethouses to Pontefract Roman road, now the A635, and it is along this ancient road that a headless horseman has been seen, emerging from the lane by St Wilfred's Church.

Ghost-hunter Terence Whitaker actually had an encounter with the horseman as a young man in 1953 when, cycling past the church, he saw a horse and rider canter up to the crossroads and vanish before his eyes. The rider was dressed in full highwayman's regalia of cloak and three-cornered hat, and so terrified Mr Whitaker that he did not stop pedalling until he reached Thurnscoe.

Just inside the lych-gate of St Wilfred's Church is a faded and dusty glass case with three heart-shaped viewing panels. Inside each of these is a human skull beneath which runs the inscription: 'Today for me; tomorrow for thee'. Several legends exist to account for the skulls and some think they may be the remains of highwaymen executed in the village, one of whom is now the headless ghost. A more prosaic explanation is given in Lockhart's *Curses,*

119

Lucks & Talismans, where it is claimed that Lord Halifax placed them there sometime in the nineteenth century 'so that inhabitants and passers-by might be reminded of the bourne to which they were travelling'.

Keen-eyed visitors to Hickleton will also notice that high on the church tower there is a very weathered example of a Celtic-style stone head gazing out across the flatlands of South Yorkshire. There is no mention of it in any of the literature dealing with the church and it appears it was placed there long ago for reasons unknown and simply forgotten about.

Goldthorpe is in the centre of South Yorkshire's mining heartland, and the popular image of miners is one of rough, tough underground men frightened of nothing – except, it seems, a ghost.

Rumours had abounded for years of there being an underground spirit at Goldthorpe colliery, and in 1985 Barry Barnett came face-to-face with something he would never forget. In an interview with the *Sheffield Star* he described exactly what happened:

I looked over the top of my newspaper and saw two miner's boots about 40ft away. As the boots came into the light I could clearly see he was wearing orange overalls. His bottom half was transparent, his top half was a silhouette. There was no head. I was frozen to the spot in fright. Goose pimples were on goose pimples.

The ghost moved towards the frightened miner but stopped just as he was about to run, fading away back into the darkness. Barry's colleagues took the sighting very seriously and NUM branch secretary Frank Calvert warned people not to ridicule the sighting, as ghosts had been seen in the pit before. It's a pity that these modern-day miners were unaware of their ancestors' techniques of dealing with underground spirits; or perhaps a well-placed sprig of rowan tree or a horseshoe may well have easily dealt with the problem.

The beautiful churchyard at the village of Aston is said to have given the poet Thomas Gray the inspiration to write his famed 'Elegy in a Country Churchyard'. The rectory at the church is now a private house known as High Trees, but the ancient building is still the haunt of a ghost, a long-forgotten rector's wife who was murdered by her husband after being found *in flagrante delicto* with the butler. Legend has it that there is still a bloodstain on the floor of the bedroom, a permanent reminder of the slaughter which can never be removed, because the blood of murdered people stains forever.

Mary Queen of Scots was imprisoned in Sheffield during the 1570s, before her execution, under the guardianship of the Earl of Shrewsbury at the Manor Lodge, which is now surrounded by a sprawling council estate. Although condemned to death she was still treated with royal occasion, often with a retinue of thirty or more servants travelling with her. While at Sheffield she was incarcerated for fourteen years in the Turret House, Sheffield being chosen because it was a remote place in those days. As with so many of her staging posts, it is alleged that her ghost returned to haunt the places of her memory and she was seen numerous times, especially in the 1930s.

Mary's ghost was seen often in the days when the Turret House was still inhabited. Terence Whitaker records a series of sightings in his *Yorkshire's Ghosts and Legends* in which a female ghost was seen both inside and outside the building. Mrs Elliot, who lived at the house during the 1930s, said:

My mother-in-law used to tell me that at twilight, one could often glance at the window and see someone, dressed in what appeared to be a cape and a cowl, peering in at them. However, on going out to investigate, no person could be found.

The Turret House, Sheffield, is said to be haunted by the ghost of Mary Queen of Scots

The Turret House is now owned by Sheffield City Council and is open to the public as a museum. Mary's ghost still appears there, and may be responsible for recent sightings of a 'grey lady' seen walking on the castellated roof.

Spring Heeled Jack is a well-known ghostly figure who terrorised the streets of London in the 1830s, but few are aware that he sprang up again in the 1870s in Sheffield. His appearances at the Cholera Monument caused panic in the city for months. The site is a monument reminding Sheffield's citizens of the cholera epidemic of 1832. A mass grave of over 400 victims lies beneath the edifice.

Sheffield historian Henry Tatton investigated the sightings and wrote that the ghost could:

> . . . spring like a goat and jump through walls and five-barred gates like a cat. It used to appear at all times of night, robed in white, and suddenly appeared in front of people, mostly courting couples, and then suddenly disappeared when anyone tried to get a hold of it.

The haunting became something of a public sensation and hundreds of people would travel to the area each night in the hope of catching sight of the bounding spectre. Gangs of youths armed with sticks and knives toured the streets hoping to confront the

Spring Heeled Jack terrified Sheffield's citizens when he appeared at the Cholera Monument in the 1870s

phantom, although they never made it clear what they would do if they managed to apprehend him.

Newspapers speculated that the ghost was just someone dressed up and pleaded, 'If an appeal made to higher feelings through the columns of a newspaper can have any effect, we beg of this "ghost" to go to Hades or to the Red Sea – or anywhere, in short, out of Norfolk Road.' If it was a mortal having fun then he or she had managed to elude the attentions of both police and lynch mobs, terrifying scores of people into the bargain, a fact lost on the sceptical newspapers of the time.

Eventually, sightings of the ghost tailed off, the last few being in the Upperthorpe area of the city, where witnesses claimed that he 'flits to and fro with meditative air, stroking a flowing beard'.

Highcliffe Road at Ecclesall has a ghost and not surprisingly, for on old maps of the area it is called Dead Man's Lane. The apparition here is of a 'white lady', first recorded in a broadsheet of 1789. A later account dating from 1873 describes a house at the head of the lane being haunted by:

> . . . a female figure robed in spectral white, without a head, flitting about the ruins, then the ghost became a barguest, with eyes as big as tea-saucers, the terror and alarm of youths of our neighbourhood.

As explained in an earlier chapter, the term 'barguest' also refers to a boggard, one of which haunts Bunting Nook, a lane on the eastern side of Graves Park near Norton church. Several writers have commented on the eerie atmosphere at Bunting Nook and it is difficult to know which came first, the atmosphere or the haunting. The Boggard of Bunting Nook either took the form of a black dog with saucer-like eyes, or in later accounts peculiar green mists which would coalesce into humanoid shapes.

Sheffield ghost-hunter Valerie Salim noted that 'the only time I've had any eerie sensations myself was walking in Bunting Nook', perhaps giving away the basis for many ghost stories when she continued, 'I'd read so much about it – and about the green human-shaped mists that people see there – and your imagination can run riot.'

It would be difficult and perhaps unwise to ascribe pure imagination to the phenomenon seen by a policeman in 1958. While walking near the junction of Hemsworth Road and Bunting Nook, the frightened constable became one in a long line of people who have seen a human shape materialise out of a sea of mist. It is also said that birds do not sing in the area.

Strange phenomena were once so common at Oughtibridge to the north of the city that a road, Boggard Lane, was named after the manifestations. Some way along the lane is a house named Asplands, which is haunted by the ghost of a woodturner who once lived there.

Champions of Robin Hood as a physical outlaw will be pleased to learn that in South Yorkshire there is at least some evidence that he was not a figment of imagination or an interpretation of the old gods.

Dodsworth, the historian, noted in 1620 that, 'Robin Locksley was born in Bradfield parish in Hallamshire, wounded his step-father to death at plough, fled to the woods and was relieved by his mother until discovered.' This passage firmly connects the outlaw with the Sheffield suburb of Loxley and the area has various landmarks named after him. A Robin Hood's Cave exists on Loxley Edge and a Robin Hood's Well can be located on Loxley Common. Other sites and place names such as Robin Hood's Bower have led generations of enthusiasts to believe this really was the birthplace of Britain's most famous outlaw.

However, as with all accounts of Robin Hood, when the surface is scratched the ballads, tales and place names seem to be disguising a far older legacy of belief and tradition.

Boggard Lane in Oughtibridge is named after the area's many strange manifestations

124

For instance, during the seventeenth century Robin Hood's Bower was a tent-like structure in which sat a man representing the king of the May games – Robin Hood – who was clothed with garlands of fresh leaves and flowers. This tradition is mentioned in church wardens' accounts of the times, along with descriptions of items of clothing for the actors who played Little John, Maid Marian and the other members of Robin's band in a yearly enactment of the 'summer game'.

The summer game was in fact a fertility ritual which took place on or around 1 May in the woods on Loxley Common. Historian S.O. Addy was convinced that while *a* Robin Hood may have been born at Loxley, he was not the source of the legends or the May games which were rooted in a far older tradition. Addy identified Hood and his men as mythological beings, with their origins in Norse and Saxon pantheons of gods, saying:

> Long after the introduction of Christianity, the old divinities, who were the only gods in the likeness of men, were not entirely driven out of popular memory, but lingered in such places as Loxley Firth and were represented by actors at the summer festival!

The ghost of Mary Revill, slain on New Year's Eve 1812 by a mysterious assailant, also stalks Loxley Common. A spate of ghost sightings in 1920 from the area described a 'woman in white who glides silently and now and again raises her arms in lament or imprecations'. Farm larbourer Clarence Swain was just one witness who remembered the ghost all too clearly.

He and his sister had been making their way to Hillsborough late one night when they saw it, Swain recounting that as they passed Myers Lane his sister screamed:

> Oh look Clar! And when I looked there was something white coming across, like a woman, maybe, holding her arms up. Then it vanished across by the old pit. It scared me right, and my sister wouldn't talk for a bit as she was very 'feared'.

Myers Lane was the scene of another encounter, this time of a UFO, when in April 1977 a couple parked in the lane witnessed a bright orange light in exactly the same place where Clarence Swain and his sister had had their experience. The strange light was emanating from a dome-shaped object which began to move rapidly towards the car. As it moved toward them the terrified couple could see a huge figure standing in the light which they described as having 'frizzy hair and furry boots'. This was too much for the pair, and the driver, Robert Holmes, started the car up and drove rapidly off. But they couldn't escape. As they sped off down the road the UFO followed them, gaining on them, even though Robert was reaching speeds of up to 75 mph.

Just as they feared the UFO was going to catch and envelope them, they passed a car parked at the side of the road and as they did so their mysterious pursuer vanished. When they looked back down the road there was no sign of the 'UFO', or indeed anything else.

The Sheffield suburb of Attercliffe was once a small country village, home to clergyman William Bloom in the seventeenth century. On 21 July 1661 he recorded in his diary that:

A most singular sight was seen at Attercliffe. A large army of soldiers dressed in white appeared, winding their way by the banks of the Don. These were followed by innumerable horsemen, mounted upon white steeds. This silent phantom army continued to pass for nearly an hour, and was attested to by many witnesses.

Other examples of ghost armies were sighted during this period all over the country, yet no one nowadays ever sees spectral columns of tanks and armoured cars. Why this is so is one more mystery to be solved in the annals of ghostlore.

On Hallam Moor on the far western boundaries of South Yorkshire stands one of the county's most enigmatic stones. The Head Stone, as it is known, towers like an Easter Island sentinel overlooking the Rivelin valley and the A57 road. On its southern side can be clearly seen the outline of a head. Originally it was known as Stump John or the Cock Crowing Stone, and S.O. Addy ascribes to it the legend that 'it is said that on a certain morning in the year these stones turn round when the sun shines on them'.

Usually public houses are grateful of a ghostly visitor for the extra custom it may bring, but so many customers at The Crofts in Mosborough complained of an apparition when the pub opened in the mid-1980s that drastic steps have been taken in an attempt to rid the hostelry of its unwanted visitor.

A pond just outside the pub seemed to be the focus for the apparition of a horse and a farm cart which dashed in front of customers parking their cars at the pub. The pond was once the only one in the area where farmers could water their animals in the evenings, and the pub car park was built over the old track leading to it. In order to end the haunting the landlord decided to fill in the pond to prevent motorists distracted by the thirsty equine ghost having an accident.

Geoff Blackburn was unconcerned about what people might think about his modern ghost-laying technique saying:

I know it sounds silly but we're hoping this will do the trick. The horse and cart has appeared so life-like to several people that they have pulled up suddenly in the car park because they believed they were going to run into it.

The enigmatic Head Stone on Hallam Moor is rumoured to turn round once a year when the morning sun shines on it

Bibliography

Alexander, M. *The Devil Hunter* (Sphere, 1978)
Ahier, A. *Legends of Huddersfield and District* (Advertiser Press, Huddersfield, 1943)
Charlton, L. *The History of Whitby* (York, 1779)
Clarke, D. *Strange Sheffield* (Priv. Pub., Sheffield, 1987)
Cooper, A. N. *Curiosities of East Yorkshire* (E. Dennis, 1935)
Cooper, J. *The Case of the Cottingley Fairies* (Hale, 1990)
Cowling, E. T. *Rombalds Way* (H. Walker, Otley, 1946)
Fairfax-Blakeborough, J. *Yorkshire Village Life* (EP Publishing, 1977)
 Yorkshire East Riding (Hale, 1951)
Green, B. *The Outlaw Robin Hood* (Kirklees Cultural Services, 1991)
Hope, R. C. *Holy Wells, their Legends and Traditions* (Stock, 1893)
Hole, C. *Haunted England* (Batsford, 1940)
Jeffrey, S. *Whitby Lore & Legend* (Anthony Rowe, 1985)
Keel, J. *Strange Creatures from Time and Space* (Sphere, 1976)
Lockhart, J. G. *Curses, Lucks & Talismans* (Maclehose, 1938)
Lofthouse, J. *Northern Country Folklore* (Hale, 1976)
Nicholson, J. *Folk Lore of East Yorkshire* (EP Publishing, 1973)
Palmer, R. *Britain's Living Folklore* (David & Charles, 1991)
Pennick, N. *Mazes and Labyrinths* (Hale, 1990)
Philips, G. R. *Brigantia* (RKP, 1976)
 The Unpolluted God (Northern Lights, 1987)
Randles, J. *The Pennine UFO Mystery* (Grafton, 1983)
Sutcliffe, H. *The Striding Dales* (Warne & Co.)
Taylor, I. *The Giant of Penhill* (Northern Lights, 1987)
Underwood, P. *This Haunted Isle* (Javelin, 1984)
Walker, P. *Folk Tales from the North York Moors* (Hale, 1990)
Watson, L. *The Nature of Things* (Hodder and Stoughton, 1990)
Whitaker, T. *North Country Ghosts & Legends* (Grafton, 1988)